Lure Coursing

Lure coursing is excitement! This wonderful phase of canine competition gives owners of sighthounds the opportunity to enjoy their animals doing what they were developed for. Here two Borzois owned by Diana Darling blaze past the camera.

Lure Coursing

Field Trialing for Sighthounds and How to Take Part

Arthur S. Beaman

HOWELL BOOK HOUSE

New York

Maxwell Macmillan Canada
Toronto

Maxwell Macmillan International
New York   Oxford   Singapore   Sydney

Copyright © 1994 by Arthur S. Beaman

Howell Book House
Macmillan Publishing Company
866 Third Avenue
New York, NY 10022

Maxwell Macmillan Canada, Inc.
1200 Eglinton Avenue East
Suite 200
Don Mills, Ontario M3C 3N1

Macmillan Publishing Company is part of the Maxwell Communication Group of Companies.

Library of Congress Cataloging-in-Publication Data
Beaman, Arthur S.
    Lure coursing : field trialing for sighthounds and how to take
part / Arthur S. Beaman.
        p.   cm.
    ISBN 0-87605-628-1
    1. Lure field trials.   2. Gazehounds.   I. Title.
SF425.55.B43   1994   93-17582
636.7'53—dc20   CIP

Macmillan books are available at special discounts for bulk purchases for sales promotions, premiums, fund-raising, or educational use. For details, contact:

Special Sales Director
Macmillan Publishing Company
866 Third Avenue
New York, NY 10022

10 9 8 7 6 5 4 3 2 1

Printed in the United States of America

To Dual Ch. Black Brants Red Ruffian, SC (Red Fox) who, at age eleven years plus, is still going strong both on the bench and in the field and was an important incentive to the writing of this book

It would be hard to say whether these Afghans or their handlers are more excited as they prepare for the start of a run.

Contents

Sighthounds have aided man in the hunt since biblical times. These Salukis are virtually unchanged from their distant ancestors that served their Arab masters from time out of mind.

Acknowledgments

To

Lin Jenkins for a wonderful chapter on Canadian coursing. Writing this chapter was almost as demanding as writing the entire book.

Vicky Clarke, editor of *Field Advisory News* (*FAN*) and the *Open Field Coursing Newsletter*, for her description of open coursing and some fantastic photographs.

Diane Houghton for her magnificent transcription of Lyle Gillette's history of lure coursing that he taped and sent to me.

Linda Garwacki for her lovely line drawings and insights into the Whippet breed.

Ruth Beaman, my wife, for her patience with me and for doing my share of our kennel work while I was writing.

The Scottish Deerhound has been known since the medieval era and was the special joy of the nobility. Essential to the sport of deerstalking, these magnificent animals captured the admiration of Sir Edwin Landseer, Sir Walter Scott and other celebrated artists and writers. *William Brown*

Preface

THOSE WHO HAVE BEEN involved in lure coursing for many years might look askance at the credentials of the author of this book, asking, Who is this person that has been coursing for just seven years? How is he qualified to write a book on the subject? This preface and a short history of my forty-five years in purebred dogs should provide a satisfactory answer to this question.

The first breed I owned was the Scottish Deerhound—back in 1947. I purchased a bitch from Stanerigg Kennels, owned by the well-known sculptress Anna Hyatt Huntington, and bred her to the best male in this country, Ch. Prophetic of Ross. She produced eight pups. Unfortunately, immunization was far less sophisticated then, and hepatitis took all but three of the litter. I was secretary of the Deerhound Club for four years and also wrote the monthly column for *Pure-Bred Dogs—American Kennel Gazette*. Things went along quietly until I moved to the West Coast in 1950 and settled in northern California, about eight miles east of Oakland in Contra Costa County. At that time, this was a wide-open county consisting of huge cattle ranches and many gambling houses and other places of ill repute. As usual, I was writing for various newspapers and doing a bit of bird hunting. As a result of the latter activity, I became friendly with the local game warden. One morning he called me and asked whether I would like to try my Deerhound, Heather, on deer. I thought he was joking as even then it was illegal in most states to use dogs to hunt deer. He explained that herds of mule deer were ravaging some of the local nurseries and doing thousands of dollars of damage every month. He had formed a small posse and thought Heather might be useful. I was interested and so the next morning, bright and early, he arrived with five others on horseback, all with rifles. He had brought a little palomino for me. I knew little about riding, but this horse knew enough for both of us. Although my Deerhound had never even seen a horse, she was undaunted and trotted off with us as if she had been doing this all her life. After about an hour our lead rider, through his field glasses, spotted a herd ambling along about a half mile ahead. Heather had spotted them already, without the help of glasses, and took off. We were actually hard put to keep up with her. Now I had done some reading on deer and Deerhounds, and I knew deer can outdistance hounds on the flat or going downhill. If the herd goes uphill, however, the hounds and horses have a good chance of catching them. To my knowledge, Heather had never even seen a deer, but she ran wide and finally succeeded in turning the herd uphill. We were about 400 yards to the rear, but I saw with my own eyes this sweet Deerhound bitch cut out a straggler from the herd and close in. Before we could catch up with her, she had brought the deer down by severing the tendons on both rear legs. She then administered the coup de grace at its throat. When I finally put a leash on her, she was munching on the choice hindquarter, looking very pleased with herself. Heather dispatched two more mule deer that day; the posse brought down the rest. They were all donated to a local hospital. All in the posse were very respectful of Heather, and several of them asked about getting a pup. When we arrived at my cottage, she entered and flopped down on her favorite couch, completely exhausted. This was my initial experience in hunting with sighthounds. As, a few years later, I was to go ''professional'' in dogs, it was also the start of an enduring interest in dual-purpose dogs regardless of breed.

I returned to the East Coast in 1951, but Heather had left her mark on the West Coast. She was the first Deerhound to be shown on the bench in California and also produced the first litter to be born in that state. She had twenty-two pups, and we saved eleven. Shortly after my return east, I met my wife, Ruth Williams, who was a top sporting-dog and terrier handler. I decided that I would also turn professional and, after studying under her for a year, finally acquired my

American Kennel Club (AKC) license to handle all breeds in the show ring. As luck would have it, we were handling a good many retrievers—Goldens, Labradors and Chesapeakes. Ruth was also breeding Goldens. In those days, dogs that were shown on the bench were also worked in the field, both for hunting and in field trials. I immediately became interested in the field part of it and have remained so to the present day.

For the next fifteen years, I showed many sporting dogs on the bench with some measure of success and also ran many of the same dogs in AKC field trials. It was difficult competing against the field-trial professionals who devoted all their time to the field, while we had to train our dogs part-time and show them as well as run them. It was challenging but also fun.

One of my own dogs was a big black Lab named Rocky. He was a handsome animal and did very well in the show ring as well as running in field trials. That started my dream of owning my own dual champion, a dream that I finally fulfilled years later with a Saluki. Retriever trials were tough, though, and Rocky was a very jumpy dog on line. Today he would be called "hyper." He thought the trials were fun because when we went out duck and goose hunting he was steady as a rock. I remember once rising at 3 A.M. and driving down to Maryland to a licensed field trial. The first test was on two shot pheasants, the first shot out about a hundred yards, the second shot off line right over the dog's head. In lure coursing much depends on the lure operator; in retriever trials, much depends on the guns. Birds have to be shot cleanly. Rocky was one of the first dogs on line. The long bird was dropped cleanly, but the one close up was wounded and, after several more shots, came to rest about two yards from my dog, squawking loudly. It was too much for Rocky. In one bound, he picked up the bird and presented it to me. In open-all-ages stakes, breaking is a disqualification, and so we were finished. Five hours down to Maryland and five hours back for one series. When I think back, it reminds me of some of the lure-coursing trials I have run in. It's painful at the moment, but you can laugh about it later.

During those fifteen years, I ran many retrievers, as well as a good number of other bird dogs in trials. We even campaigned a homebred Beagle for a short time. For at least ten years, my wife was the top sporting-dog handler in the United States. We usually had eight or nine Bests in Show dogs in our string of campaigners, and it was hard work.

During this period I started the Westchester Retriever Field Trial Club mainly to get some people to help me train my dogs. That club, of which I was president for four years, is still holding AKC-licensed field trials each year. However, things were getting tighter and tighter in Rye, New York, where our kennel was located, and when the town finally passed an ordinance prohibiting the shooting of firearms within village limits, it spelled the end for us. We put our large kennel on the market, sold it and moved to central New York, where we are still located. At the same time, we both retired as professional handlers and concentrated on training various breeds for the field while I continued to be very active in writing for various magazines about dogs. In 1979, my wife brought home a four-month-old bundle of white fluff—a Saluki pup—that was to signal a big change in my life. I was used to ordering dogs around; now I found myself in the reverse position. Even my Deerhound, who paid no attention to anyone but me, was obedient. Not Jambi, our first Saluki. I had just finished my first book, *The Chesapeake Bay Retriever*, and when my publisher asked me to do a book on the Saluki, we decided to breed a litter. Fortunately, Don Weiden, one of the most knowledgeable Saluki breeders in the country, lived nearby and we were fortunate enough to be able to breed to his multichampion Jen Araby Mahal Bey. After the breeding, Don invited us in to his house. We left Jambi uncrated in the car, and that was a mistake. When we came out, we found that she had chewed the upholstery on both sides of the wagon and on all the seats. However, she did produce a beautiful litter and we kept three—two boys and a girl. I went to work on my Saluki book, but I began to realize that I didn't know enough at that time, and so I decided to discontinue the project. It was a wise decision.

For the first few years of our new puppies' lives, I was working full time for a veterinarian and also writing for several magazines. This meant that I didn't have much time for our new brood. I also had several health problems of my own that came close to ending my career abruptly. But I survived, and one day as I was walking my red Saluki (Red Fox), I took a close look at him. He looked so handsome that I suddenly decided to go back in the show ring after an absence of some twenty years and make him a champion. It was easier than I thought it would be. The same bunch of amateurs were around, grousing about the professionals instead of learning how to handle their dogs, and Red Fox went through the breed in four months and a dozen shows to his championship. Then in the late fall of 1986, someone invited me down to a "fun" trial for sighthounds. This, believe it or not, was the first time I had ever heard of lure coursing. The American Sighthound Field Association had kept it a secret, at least from me. I took two of our boys down, Red Fox and Rabbit. Rabbit didn't do very well, but Red Fox chased the "bunny" as though he was born for it. It was love at first sight. I think it was the first time he had been off lead since he was a year old. At that time, I used to let my dogs run. One morning the Fox was missing. I eventually found him calmly walking around on the roof. Evidently he had jumped on to the roof of the porch first and had then made his way up the slanting roof the way a mountain goat would. Needless to say, that was the last time I let him off lead, at least until he started coursing. After several near-disasters, one coursing-related and one not, that put him on the shelf for six months, he finally finished, and I had my first dual champion after forty years of trying.

Since then, I have finished others and failed with quite a few. I still keep trying though, partly because I enjoy it, but mostly because my dogs enjoy it. This will be my third book. The first was written in Belgium at the tail end of World War II; the second didn't appear until 1981. I think I have the credentials to write this one, and I hope that you both read and enjoy it. I tried to put in something for both the novice and the experienced lure courser, and I think I succeeded. I hope you think so, too.

Tallahamra Mithers Zan-Jabil, CC, CM, a Saluki in hot pursuit of the game at the Grand Course, 1992. *Bryan Wilson*

Closing in for the kill. *Lou Lockren*

1

The Forerunner—
Open-Field Coursing

LYLE GILLETTE was the inventor of lure coursing, but his fame and expertise did not start with that invention. In the early 1960s, Gillette also started what is known today as open-field coursing. In this sport, the sighthounds are released on various types of live rabbits, usually Jacks, but sometimes on European hare. Borzois were Lyle Gillette's first love, and so this breed once known as the Russian Wolfhound was the first to run in open-field coursing. Soon after, the Saluki and other sighthounds joined in the sport. The main difficulties in open coursing lie in finding enough rabbits and finding fields with a limited number of fences and other obstacles that might cause injury to the hounds. In fact, by 1970 Gillette himself had concluded that open coursing was too risky, and so he turned his fertile brain to work inventing a substitute. In 1972, he came up with lure coursing and became the first president of the American Sighthound Field Association (ASFA).

Open-field coursing is still practiced, although it is now limited to a few states in the Southwest and far West, due to the number of rabbits needed and the open territory available. I am deeply indebted to Vicky Clarke for the following description of open-field coursing.

Vicky is the editor of both *Field Advisory News (FAN)*, the official voice of ASFA, and *NOFCA News*, the official voice of the National Open Field Coursing Association.

A formal open-field competition (generally referred to as a "hunt") is conducted very much like a lure trial. A specific location and time (usually 6 A.M. to 7 A.M.) is designated where the entrants meet for roll call and draw. Roll call is held to determine the hounds present, whether any of the bitches are in season, and to inspect them all for soundness. It is usually held outside a restaurant, and those involved have breakfast while this is happening. Entry for hunts varies. If there are more than twenty in attendance and the hunt has been advertised in advance, entry can be split into two fields. Otherwise they break after twenty-seven. If split, the fields are somewhat evenly balanced, bearing in mind how many hares it will take to support the field (in other words, if it means an extra rabbit, one will be lopsided in order to save an extra run/hare). Hounds run in trios or braces, depending on the quantity. If, after being in the field a long time, the hare seem to be scarce, runs can be combined to make four dog courses—running yellow, pink, blue and unblanketed as a bye dog.

The hounds and handlers who are hunting (on the line) walk in front or at one end of the gallery (all other participants are conducted into formation by the huntmaster). The gallery is urged to pay attention, stay in order, and walk slowly through the fields, calling attention to any hare they see with a direction. This direction is given for the huntmasters' and handlers' sake so they can try to sight their hounds before releasing them. The directions used are, Rabbit left! Rabbit right! Rabbit front! Rabbit behind! (or whatever the excited gallery members can blurt out!). Huntmasters usually call the rabbit and direction; however they only have to give the *tallyho* (to start the hounds). It all depends on how fast things are happening, how fast the rabbits are, how far away they are breaking, and so on. The main difference between lure coursing and open-field coursing is that in the latter hounds are given only a preliminary run. The hound has to win its course or meet the average of the course winners in order to be brought up into final competition. Some judges are more lenient than others about bringing dogs up, but that, too, depends upon the time of day, the supply of hare, and other considerations. If you are interested in open-field coursing, write to Vicky Clarke, *NOFCA News*, P.O. Box 399, Alpaugh, CA 93201, for further information.

If most or all of the foregoing seems like Greek to you, please

Tallahamra Musdiy, CC, CM, was rated number one for 1990 and 1991 by the National Open Field Coursing Association. This Saluki and its trophy were photographed by Susan Schroder.

bear with me and you will shortly learn the regulations for lure coursing. Dogs running in open coursing today almost have to be familiar with hazards, especially barbed-wire fences. That, and the fact that the sport is limited geographically, also limits the number of participants. Although the American Kennel Club always encouraged this type of coursing, it understood its limitations and therefore could never sanction it. In fact, it was not until the ASFA had been in existence for twenty years that the American Kennel Club decided that the sport of lure coursing had become popular enough for it to establish its own program.

Never lose sight of the lure.   *Newton*

2

Lyle Gillette on the History of Lure Coursing

IF LYLE GILLETTE is not a household word in the United States today, it is not his fault. Lure coursing has remained a comparatively small outdoor sport, limited first by the rather small number of sighthounds available to take part and second by the reluctance or inability of the parent organization to bring the sport to the attention of the American public. Lure coursing is not only a great participant sport but also one of the best spectator sports going on today. In a small way with our own coursing club, I have been able to inform some of the public and they turned out to see the hounds run. Many who had never been to a trial before were so enthusiastic they asked about acquiring a sighthound so they could participate. Almost all asked when the next trials would be held so they could come out and watch.

Lyle Gillette was the beginning of all this almost thirty years ago. Years before that he ran one of the top Beagle field-trial clubs in California and so much of the terminology for lure coursing, such as huntmaster, tallyho, and many others, comes down from the Beagle trials. Lyle spent almost half his adult life organizing, first, open-field coursing and, then, lure coursing in their present forms.

Everything has a beginning. Sometimes that beginning is not recognizable, but we have to deal with what we remember. The beginning of my wanting to do something for sighthounds was when I discovered that there was such a thing as a sighthound. We had Beagles at that time, and I believe that I discovered sighthounds simultaneously with my realization that there were also scent hounds. I was active in the Beagle club and in Beagle work in general. Nearly forty years ago, we organized a Beagle club in Santa Clara Valley, here in California. We called it the Boston Valley Beagle Club. It's still one of the outstanding Beagle clubs in the United States. We organized the Beagle Club at first so that we'd have some common meeting ground on which to work with our hounds, to understand them better so that we'd be able to raise Beagles properly. This is what anybody who handles animals—whether Beagles or whatever—wants, but we also knew that you could do better if you organized around your breed—got a number of people to form an organization and then built up communications, built up joint activity so that everybody could exchange experience. Well, this was on its way when I began to discover the idea of field trials and how valuable they were for the dogs and particularly sighthounds.

Throughout history, dog breeds were developed to fill specific needs. Herding dogs were developed to herd and protect livestock and, in some cases, to guard property. Similarly, sighthounds were brought into existence by human beings for a purpose, and they proved themselves admirably suited to that purpose. Man didn't evolve sighthounds just because it was something to do—these hounds were an asset to his means of survival and gave him his livelihood. If he lived where there was game, he had to catch the game. Many years before the invention of firearms, dogs that would hunt were the means to capture game. Even with bow hunting, dogs were still used to a great extent. As time went on, dogs began to be used for more and more varied tasks. Ancient tribes used coursing hounds to catch game in the course of their travels. As time went on, more dog breeds, performing more and more specialized tasks, became established. Guide dogs for the blind became perfected over time from existing breeds as hearing and therapy dogs. At one time this was the underlying reason for all dogs. This use and evolution of dogs always intrigued me. Why couldn't our own dogs do the work that their predecessors did? In the case of sighthounds, for example, who kept sighthounds to run game down? No one! For years, game laws in most places have restricted the use of dogs on wild animals. On top of that, many wild-animal species were killed off by man after the invention of firearms. Man and his weapons have repeatedly wiped out many species. For instance, at one time the passenger pigeon existed by the millions in the United States; now there isn't a single one left on earth, wiped out by man and the profit motive. Nothing was done to protect and perpetuate the species. So many game animals that have disappeared helped to perfect and maintain sighthounds and other animals that we had trained to meet specific needs. Their jobs or specialties were eliminated because what they did was no longer needed or the game they pursued was no longer available.

So we came into active participation through Beagles. I got interested in watching Beagles working the fields. We would go out on the weekend, spend two days in Beagle field trials, two and three times a year, and it would be a complete family outing. We'd go out to the field-trial area and set up tents, trailers, shelter and cooking facilities along with every other necessity for the whole weekend. Many people enjoyed this more than fishing trips or similar outdoor sports. They had dogs they loved, so this is what they did. I got acquainted with the Beagle crowd then, but, at the same time, we also had Borzois— more for their aristocratic beauty than their utility or sport. I used to love to take a Borzoi walking in San Francisco or in some of the smaller villages around San Francisco. Before I'd gone a block, three or four people would have stopped me to ask questions about my dog's breed. I would explain that Borzois had been used to hunt wolves and other game by the aristocracy in czarist Russia. I related the tales I'd heard about their prowess as hunters during these encounters. I used to brag about their ability to do this sort of thing, but at the same time I'd wonder if Borzois today could do what their ancestors did after a life of luxury and pampering for the past century. All these dogs ever saw of the outside world was their view from the window. No one would turn a hound loose—they were afraid it would start running and get so excited it would get lost and never be able to find its way back home. So the hound was pretty much confined to the backyard, the house, and wherever his owner might want to take him.

I became more and more curious about whether Borzois were capable of doing the things they were bred to do. And not only Borzois. There were at that time seven other recognized sighthound breeds. I knew people with Whippets, Afghans and Salukis that could certainly benefit from getting involved in coursing. As curiosity about sighthounds grew it mounted to a point where I felt that I had to do something about it since no one else was. After the field trials were over one weekend, I took a couple of old Borzoi bitches I owned out in the field with me, thinking, "I wonder what they could do with a rabbit?" I helped them scare up a rabbit, and they took a look at it. You could tell they wanted to chase it, but they didn't know whether that was the thing to do. I tried to coax them into it, but they didn't get the idea of what to do until the rabbit was out of sight. We walked on over the field a little farther and got up another rabbit. Well, this time *I* ran after the rabbit. Of course I caught up with it right away, but the rabbit disappeared from sight almost as quickly as if I hadn't followed it at all, and this gave the dogs the idea that I was trying to chase it. One hound ran out quite a bit farther after the rabbit and then lost sight of it. I said, "Well, I'll put an end to this." I had my shotgun along with me. I had brought it because I dreamed about such a condition developing. I said to the hounds, "Well, we'll scare one up, and I'll shoot it." We walked a little farther, and up came a hare, and I didn't wait for it to go out of sight. I shot it right away and then tied the rabbit carcass to a rope and made a drag. The hound chased it immediately, and I got it moving fast enough so that I could swing it out around me and I had those old gals chasing that rabbit in a circle around me as I spun it on the end of the rope. That gave them a little taste of rabbit blood and a feel for catching the thing. They realized then what it was about.

After this experience, we struck out again and got up another rabbit, this one in an area with weeds, grass and cover. The hounds got a good sighting of the hare and took after it, giving it a real good, sound chase, and they enjoyed it tremendously. They came back in and were panting and blowing for all they were worth, but you could tell by looking at them that they had had a ball. "Boy, this is what I love to do," they seemed to proclaim. And when I saw that sparkle in their eye and then how pleased and how happy they appeared, to be able to have that little spurt of exercise. I thought, "Well, they've done enough for today. I'm going to load them up and go home." I was tired anyway, so we went home, and I spent that night telling my wife all about it.

On the following weekend, I decided to continue my experiment. Before daylight, I took three dogs out—one male along with the two

To the Borzoi, coursing through snow-covered fields comes naturally.

Despite its commanding size, a Borzoi has the ability to change direction in an instant to keep up with an elusive prey.

15

bitches—and right away we got a hare up. Of course, only the bitches had had the experience from the week before, but the male didn't seem to need much coaching. He saw what to do, and when we started, he realized how much fun this was going to be. We chased up three or four rabbits that day and had a really good time. I enjoyed it even though it was just myself and the dogs. I like to be with people and wanted to share this newly discovered pleasure with others.

I thought it over when I got home and discussed it again with my wife. She became very enthusiastic about what I was doing, and so we got two other couples to go out with us the next time—about two or three weeks later. We each had a dog and just wanted to take turns running them. Our friends had fun; the dogs had fun. Everybody enjoyed it, and we knew we really had something special. We had a picnic lunch with us and stayed out all day. The rabbits weren't so numerous that we'd overtax the dogs. We'd get a rabbit up, and the dogs would do a run. Then they'd rest and we would get another one up, and then it started all over again. The dogs were taking the exercise very well, even though they had been living a soft life at home so long.

Everybody was very pleased with the day's events, so we talked it over out in the field and decided, "Let's give this a real chance. In a couple of weeks, let's get eight, ten people to come with their hounds. We'll take turns running the dogs, and everybody will participate in getting the hare up for the other guy; we'll work in an organized fashion." This we did and the next outing was a complete success. We had a lot of fun in the morning because we did the running early to avoid the full heat of the summer sun in the area. During the summer, it is better not to run sighthounds at all. We'd let them relax in the shade and keep cool because they can't take much heat and do a lot of heavy running.

Along about noon, we decided it was time to eat lunch and relax, so we started for home. Between the San Joaquin Valley, where we ran the dogs, and the Santa Clara Valley, where we all lived, there is a nice range of picturesque mountains. We stopped en route on the grassy bank of a little water course we call Pacheco Creek. Beside this stream and in it there grows a lot of watercress. Here we refreshed ourselves and gathered wild watercress. But on this pleasant day, we had a serious purpose in mind. We discussed how we could put on a simulated field trial as we learned more about the sport. And there were so many questions—How could we launch this? How should we proceed? We needed a system to get entry fees, arrange for judging and draft rules. All these questions came up, plus many more. We made a lot of temporary assignments. One young man volunteered to chair our newborn provisional committee. Another became secretary, and still others took other assignments as required. We got them involved in this first step of developing the organization. Everyone was so enthused that they just jumped at the chance to do whatever was asked of them. We developed field trials for sighthounds, and called them the Pacheco Hunt. We thought that was rather dramatic because the organization had been formed at that picnic on the banks of Pacheco Creek. So the romantic members of our group got to name it and we were the Pacheco Hunt for our first two years.

In the meantime, we communicated with the American Kennel Club about field trials and AKC recognition of them for sighthounds. The initial query concerned the Borzois because this was our breed interest. The AKC responded by advising that it would never consider sanctioning a field trial just to accommodate a rare breed like the Borzoi. They felt that other breeds should be included to make the activity stronger, get more people involved and above all, to make it more financially self-sustaining. Then the activity could finance itself because a certain amount of cost was involved, and a small group of people couldn't carry it. With several sighthound breeds involved, it would be possible to make coursing pay its own way.

All right, so we wrote rules and procedures and at the suggestion of the American Kennel Club, we invited fanciers of Afghans, Salukis, Irish Wolfhounds, Scottish Deerhounds, Greyhounds and Whippets to become part of a joint organization. The purpose was to establish field trials as a means of testing the abilities of the hounds to a point where the American Kennel Club would sanction field championships for sighthounds. That became our goal—field trials sanctioned by the American Kennel Club for the purpose of establishing field champions as with some of the other Sporting hound breeds.

That was the central issue around which coursing developed, but, as the AKC pointed out to begin with, we had a hard time spreading our message to all fifty states. It was necessary for sighthound fans in all fifty states to participate in order to keep things going. But game is limited, suitable terrain is limited, and some state laws prohibit the use of dogs to pursue live game. Our potential for activity was therefore pretty badly restricted. We were limited to about a dozen or so states where coursing was legal. If we could develop or even start an organization in each of them, we still wouldn't have enough members to carry the financial load because certain built-in expenses—judges, advertising needs, and a host of ongoing expenses of all kinds. As enthusiasts proceed and participate in coursing activities, it becomes clear how many of this and how much of that is needed, and it all costs money.

It was evident to me that something had to be done, and I, of course, felt responsible. I had started the movement and therefore felt that I should be the one to push it. The time came when the hounds in the normal course of hunting were running through fences, chasing a rabbit because they (the hounds) didn't hunt far enough away from the fences so there could be a good chance to pursue the game without having to go through barbed wire. Wire that is used to contain stock has barbs all over it, and if a hound hits that fence just right, it would just rip open the skin, particularly Whippets. I've seen their skin torn like calico cloth; you couldn't believe it. You'd think the poor animal would die, as the wounds seemed so severe and this would happen out in the field, miles away from any veterinarian. Coursers would bring along needles and thread and, while the wound was still fresh, sew the flesh back together before it became too tender and treat it with an ordinary disinfectant. None of the injured dogs I knew died from these wounds, but they were left with some hideous scars. Both Greyhounds and Whippets are very susceptible to flesh tears that will scar them for life. By comparison, coated hounds fared better. The hair on these hounds comes back and covers the scars.

At this time, we had champion Borzois and a good strain of breeding. We didn't want to take them out to run and risk getting them torn up. We tried to keep our hounds safe as much as we could. That was primarily in the minds of most people with show dogs. They didn't want to take their hounds to where their legs or feet could be broken, or their hide torn and scarred. It developed into a real hazard since with a fracture it's so seldom that a bone is ever set so true that the break is invisible after healing.

With ever more crowding of the fences, we had more wounds and more problems. Finally, we involved other organizations officially into our group and set up a central body—what we called an advisory committee. We took up the safety issue and discussed it, but no one seemed to want to do anything about it. When I went back to my own club, the Mission Valley Borzoi Club, I proposed that we get farther away from the fences and when a pursued hare went through a fence, call the chase off. From then on there was no judging of the run on the course. The club accepted the proposal and put it into the rules of that one trial. The usual crowd appeared, and the weather for the trial was good. Everyone wanted to get out, and some ninety hounds turned out to run that one day. We had to split the field into two stakes. The idea of having more than one stake in the day came about due to the overflow of entries at this one trial. When the trial was in progress, a few rabbits went through the fences, and the rules provided that the judging must stop when that happened. All the judges stopped judging, and the huntmaster told the people to pick up their hounds. The first time it happened, some of those who had brought in Greyhound racetrack rejects complained bitterly because we stopped the run over the bunny-through-the-fence rule. To us it was a safety precaution for the hounds, but these ''sportsmen'' seemed especially eager to kill a rabbit. To my mind this segment stood for mayhem, and if coursing was going to drift in such a direction, I didn't want much to do with it. The club ruling for that one trial was challenged, and a special committee meeting was held to hear the complaints. As a result the committee upheld those complaints. I told those present at the meeting that if they were ''going to allow the dogs to tear themselves up, break themselves up, whatever, I can no longer participate because I started this thing and I didn't realize the consequences.''

Often, when a hound was released, I felt responsible for its safety. If it got hurt, I would blame myself, thinking that if I hadn't started the coursing thing, the hound probably wouldn't have been hurt. In the long run, it probably would have been worse off because it wouldn't have gotten the exercise. At that time, many hounds were dying at eight and nine years of age while hounds that were given enough exercise lived to age eleven, twelve and thirteen years. They did get bruised up a bit, but in the long run they were better off for their physical conditioning. However, I didn't feel as though I wanted the responsibility on my shoulders of starting something that could be hazardous to sighthounds or any other animal. So when the club refused to accept the ruling to avoid the fences, we placed a time limit on how long the hounds could run before it was called a course. If the hounds ran through a fence before the time was up, it was declared automatically a no course. If the hounds ran longer than the allotted time and ran through the fence, it was not necessarily a no-course but the judging was stopped as soon as the hare went through the fence. So the huntmaster would order the hounds picked up and sometimes it was possible to prevent them from going into the fence at all. It all depended on how well they were trained and how accustomed they were to coming back. To a certain extent, the reliability of the return was related to the hound's breed. Some breeds come back better than others.

All through our experiences with getting lure coursing started, we were beginning something new with everything we did. Every day, every lesson was a new beginning, so we discovered that coursing does not essentially hinge on any one specific point but on a multitude of factors and on how well we put them together as a unit and made them work. Surely, we had trouble in the beginning, but we were able to start coursing and brought about an exciting, competitive activity that will endure as long as hounds run. I think that there are other things that we need to include on the modern development of sport with sighthounds.

THE SHIFT TO LURE COURSING

We held our first lure trials about two years after I withdrew from open-field coursing. I had devoted every spare moment I had, trying to bring together the equipment and any materials and ideas that I thought would work. Two people would operate a "pulley," a string that would control the lure without breaking. The right pulley couldn't create so much friction and drag as to burn out the motor and this was up to the free action of the pulley.

There were many problems that we coped with and struggled to solve to bring lure coursing to where it is today. One of the first improvements we made was in the continuous loop. This was done by a committee I appointed, from among our original board of directors, to work on and stabilize lure-coursing equipment. The development of the continuous loop was important since it allowed us to use our time to better advantage. It shortened the trials tremendously, thus allowing us to run more dogs with greater ease. With the old take-up reel, we had to restring the pulleys each time, but now only occasionally does a pulley need restringing. When something gets in the way and jerks the string off a pulley restringing is needed, but that's about as bad as it gets with a continuous loop. Then we found that it naturally took more tension to run the continuous loop, so the line had to be doubled in strength. This now meant having a spool large enough to accommodate all of the line and then if it had to be brought in to a take-up machine, the reel had to be able to take all this heavy twine and bring

Bitterblue's Balderdash, SC, F. Ch., an accomplished Whippet.   *Jenny Philips*

Ben Haasin's No Surrender, F. Ch., combines dynamic speed with breedy Afghan glamour.

it in onto one wheel. So that was a problem that was solved. There were even wheels for this purpose. That was easy enough as wheels are not too hard to make with the help of a jigsaw and people who know how to balance such equipment.

We introduced many innovations like that. One was the use of the continuous loop. The other was the time gate. With this device, as the hounds passed a certain point in the run, they were clocked. There would be three people also monitoring runs—one for each blanket color. That person would record the time of the dog wearing the color for which the timer was responsible. Since this was to determine how fast the dogs were running, we considered it particularly important in lure coursing. At first some of us thought the use of time gates would be a way to measure speed, but we soon realized that the hound closest to the judges would go through the time gate in a much shorter time than would the dog that was following the lure reel closer to the pulley. It would take this dog much longer to go from one end of the time gate to the other. So it turned out that the time gate wasn't a contribution at all. We carried it for one summer and then, the next time the rules changed, we wiped out the use of time gates.

The original racing colors we used were red, white and black, but as time went on, it was thought that iridescent colors would be easier to see from a distance. To a point this is correct, but even with iridescent colors, one could still not read the numbers perfectly in certain light or under certain conditions. That remains a problem today. We're still not sure we're reading the right blanket sometimes, especially if we're running a trial that is say, 660 yards or so and the judges have to be run into the field. If the judges are standing back from the line of coursing, their view can be distorted. Whippets in particular, with their small blankets, can be very hard to see. Sometimes the colors can be confused, and one dog will get credit for what another did because the judges get their colors confused. That doesn't happen too often, but the potential definitely exists. Disputes in most such cases are settled to the satisfaction of all parties concerned, however.

The requirements for championships also cause problems at times. We decided to require so many points and certain conditions for the title; any hound acquiring the points and meeting the conditions would be considered a field champion. Well we were making champions pretty fast, and sighthound people who lived in densely populated areas had a problem. A kennel full of dogs established in a city or town is an awkward matter. Someone may have as many as three or four dogs, but any more than that can result in trouble with neighbors. Such coursing fans often own one or two hounds that earned championships in trials but they still want to run them and participate. They can either get rid of the champions they have to make room for new dogs or quit the game. A better solution to this concern was the establishment of another rating, a program to allow field champions an outlet to continue coursing. I think the AKC's approach is a good one: a championship is the best you can get and you should have to work to get the points. Accordingly, we stretch the courses out, make them more of a test and require greater performance from the hounds. There won't be as many champions (you might call them ''cheap'' champions). It's just too easy to finish a champion now. If the dog's got a little enthusiasm and happens to chase a lure a couple of times—and the judge likes the way the hound performed—it gets high scores and away it goes. First thing you know, it's a champion. Now hounds and owners must work harder for the title. I think as the AKC progresses with its lure-coursing program, the requirement will become more difficult. People will really have to get serious and condition their hounds to win these championships. As with gun dogs, whose training requires hours, days and weeks, working with sighthounds also takes time. You've got to work with your hound and know its ability to learn and how it responds to all your effort. By the time it gets its field championship, it's earned it, and its human partner that put it through the program has also earned it. Both are in line for a good, solid reward. That is more than we can say about the present champions with the current rules, and the means of granting titles; that is, as far as the American Sighthound Field Association is concerned. ASFA must move forward to stay in this competition. It must move up there and move the distance of the runs. It must change the runs so they're more natural . . . like the natural path of a pursued rabbit trying to escape. It must simulate all the irregularities the hounds can run into in the field. Somehow it must adjust as many courses as possible to learn everything it can about how hounds perform under a variety of conditions.

The ASFA can accomplish wonderful things with some goal setting and good hard work. To many coursers, having a field champion matters most. Regardless, these dogs get exercise and make excellent use of the opportunities they have. They're also proving to the best of their abilities, as much as the environment allows, that they can do what they were bred to do. To really succeed, lure coursing needs to attract people and keep them interested. People continue on the basis of their interest in how well the hounds are trained, what kind of tests they are able to stand up to, and the requirements for field championship. Of course, dogs that win their championships under more severe conditions become valuable breeding stock. There's much about lure coursing that tells us things about our hounds we might not otherwise know. For example, in the show ring, handlers know how to control dogs—to get a certain response. They know under what conditions a dog will remain calm and obey, and so they try to maintain those conditions when they're showing the dog. As long as they are successful, the judge won't be able to judge temperament. And so a dog with a bad temperament may win over a dog that's just as good and has a better temperament but maybe doesn't carry its head as high or show some other characteristic that the judge happens to favor.

Lure coursing, on the other hand, reveals the disposition of the particular hound. Because it's got to be out in the field all day long in close contact with all kinds of other hounds, it's got to have a good temperament. Believe me, when you're in the field, you don't want to have to keep a death grip on your hound all day. It's tiring enough just to work with a hound in a field trial situation. You want a dog that obeys all the way through—temperament you can rely upon. You don't want to see your hound go halfway and then turn around and start fighting or cause a donnybrook out on the field. In the old days, if a dog started a fight with one or more of its hunting mates, in the field, it probably didn't get up the next morning for the next hunt. Its owners buried it because there wasn't enough game and those old hunters didn't have the time to fool around with some idiot dog that wanted to fight rather than hunt. So it helps in lure coursing, as with field trials, to improve the disposition of your hounds whenever you can.

That's some of what we learned just from the disposition of the dogs alone. We also wanted to have a format the AKC would accept as a test because we wanted to test the conformation of a good running hound. What type of pasterns would best be able to absorb the shock and pressure of a hard day's run? Should the front legs be straight up and down like an arrow, should they knuckle over a bit, should they bend backward some? What was the ideal?

Stamina of the hound is also critical. Stamina is somewhat related to condition, but also depends on how well the respiratory system works. Is it adequate to furnish all the oxygen required by a hound during the stress of a hard chase? Does a slab-sided Borzoi do better in the field than one with a slight spring of rib? I think the dog with some rib spring will have more stamina than a slab-sided dog, and this is the Borzoi that the Standard calls for—spring creates both more lung space to pull oxygen in and even more space for the heart to function. So that requirement in the Standard is correct.

I don't know of anything detrimental in any breed Standard, though I have some reservations. I'm not an Irish Wolfhound breeder, but I've observed them for some years. I feel as though those who are breeding Irish Wolfhounds are demanding too much size. They are not meant to carry such large frames. The result is the Irish Wolfhound's very short life span. Most live only eight or nine years or less and these are considered old dogs. There is not a great deal of difference between a tall Greyhound and a good-sized Borzoi. A good-sized Borzoi will live thirteen to fifteen years and Greyhounds will live that long or longer because they haven't outgrown the ability of their frames to do that which is demanded of the hounds. So much good can come from coursing dogs as far as interpreting the Standards of the sighthound breeds is concerned. All of this activity pulls together the conformation dog, the working dog, the coursing dog, the gun dog. All of this is part of the whole dog game, and the show is also just a part of the dog game.

What I have been trying to do is to point out the value of lure coursing or any kind of coursing, working your hounds. What is it? I think it can be summed up thus: It creates a more durable animal. The animal is stronger, can run farther, looks better and is more agile. We consider it necessary that it possess a certain amount of intelligence, of course, because if it didn't have that it wouldn't be able to course. So on and on we go in summing up the many facets of the good that comes from using our hounds in the field.

Now that the American Kennel Club has accepted lure coursing as part of its performance-events program, I want to repeat that at the first meeting of our lure-coursing enthusiasts, the preamble to our work, our purpose for existence was expressed in the purpose of the organization. We were going to develop a system of trials to test our hounds' ability to do the work their ancestors did. We hoped the American Kennel Club would feel right in taking up our program and pushing it forward as part of its own program. At every convention from the first to the tenth, there were motions on the floor reiterating and restating that our central purpose was to get AKC recognition so that the future of coursing would be assured. We wanted the benefits that derive from having your dogs published in the various records of the American Kennel Club. So we fought and worked to get a system that the AKC would accept as a means of testing the hounds and, in 1991, the American Kennel Club ran its first lure trials, not by ASFA's rules, but reflecting some of the practices of some leaders of the American Sighthound Field Association.

At the time, this was pretty much my lifetime goal. I knew when I started to organize a system that the American Kennel Club could eventually accept it. I knew that it wouldn't come about overnight, that there would have to be a lot of effort put into it. We had to first find a system that would really test the dogs. We had to show that there was a chance of the thing paying its own way because everything that the AKC accepts has to pay its own way. Who else is going to finance it? You might get a few donations from here and there but, in general, the financing has to come out of the pockets of the people who raise and sell and show and join in the activity of the dogs and dog shows. When we proved that we could finance the activity, the AKC wasn't reluctant to accept lure coursing. In fact, AKC accepted the format on its own. We didn't have to beg. It could see the value of it, so AKC moved right along and went ahead regardless of opposition.

Now we have two lure-coursing organizations. When the coursing issue came up at the convention I was asked: "What are we going to do now?" I said, "The AKC is going to course dogs and we're going to course dogs, and we're both going to do everything that we can to promote coursing, not to promote a fight between the American Kennel Club and the remnants of the American Sighthound Field Association. We're going to work to bring people together—bring together the dogs, the people, the effort, the fun, and the principle of the thing—and when we've done that, we'll find that there is one general center for coursing activity. And it's my bet that it will be the American Kennel Club."

All those who realize what value coursing has for hounds will decide that coursing is what we're going to do, no matter what label we give to it, and we're going to make the courses as natural as possible. In doing this, we will get the bulk of people who are interested in coursing for sport, particularly those who are interested in it because of the way it benefits dogs.

When I found out that the American Kennel Club was going to start running field trials, I felt that my mission in life was pretty much fulfilled. This was what I had been working for for thirty years, and it had come to pass. The fact that the ASFA and the AKC still weren't seeing eye to eye didn't bother me at all because I know that the AKC is into coursing. I knew that there are a lot of people within the ASFA that will not allow the thing to develop into a fight between ASFA and the AKC because they know that cooperation will lead to better and bigger field trials. No ifs about it—that's the only way it can go. So I'm very proud to have been associated with a movement that has had so much success in such a short time. Only twenty years ago, we pulled the first lure through the pulleys and now the American Kennel Club is going to put on a field trial, a sanctioned field trial. And that's a pretty good step. You go back into the history of other activities, dogs and otherwise, you don't find developments like that taking place as rapidly as it did with this thing. This was a new approach to a whole big problem that had been lying in wait for a hundred and fifty years. Poor old sighthounds were sleeping on the rugs at home. Their muscles were soft, they were bored, and they died young. Some of them were skin and bone and others so fat they could hardly walk. All this was because they had nothing to live for. They had no excitement and weren't able to practice the things most natural to them. Lure coursing has put an end to that. Take a look at the hounds that were in the show ring twenty years ago and look at the sighthounds in the show ring now. You'll see that all the breeds have progressed and become better animals, better structured, just all around better flesh and blood creatures than those that existed before because there was no use for them. I am proud to have had a part in all this.

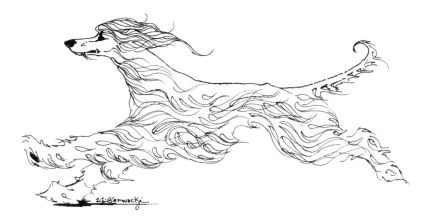

Lure coursing provides a competitive ground for all running hounds, and all eligible breeds participate with great enthusiasm.

3

Who May Run— The Eligible Breeds

AT THIS WRITING, there are eleven eligible breeds according to the ASFA and the AKC. The latter organization recognized the Rhodesian Ridgeback as the eleventh eligible breed on September 1, 1992, the former in April 1993.

Afghan Hounds, Basenjis, Borzois, Greyhounds, Ibizan Hounds, Irish Wolfhounds, Pharaoh Hounds, Rhodesian Ridgebacks, Salukis, Scottish Deerhounds and Whippets make up the list of breeds.

In this chapter, it would be impossible to give a detailed history of each breed without writing almost a full book. Therefore each history will be necessarily brief with the Standard conforming to the official Standard written by the parent clubs of each breed and approved by the American Kennel Club. The profiles that follow should whet your appetite, hone your perceptions and provide you with a greater appreciation of your own breed and all the other "running hounds."

THE AFGHAN HOUND

This versatile hound, as its name implies, originated in Afghanistan and is used for hunting almost all types of game, including fox,

The Afghan Hound is a mountain runner whose conformation was especially suited to the environment in its place of origin. Its long, beautiful coat protected it from all extremes of weather. The breed has adapted well to lure coursing and is supported by an enthusiastic field following.

gazelle, rabbit and even birds if the hunter so desires. The Afghan is one of the original breeds recognized by ASFA for lure coursing. They also participated in open-field coursing before the lure originated and a small number of Afghans still do. The Afghan does not have the speed of some other sighthounds, such as the Saluki and the Greyhound, but it is very agile and can take unexpected turns without running excessively wide, as Greyhounds often do. It has excellent endurance and recovers quickly after an arduous course.

Many Afghan owners clip their dogs, but I have seen several running in full coat and it didn't seem to make a great deal of difference. I had the pleasure of running for several years at many trials with a beautiful black Afghan bitch who was the top-scoring Afghan in the country in 1988. She was a pleasure to watch and had an excellent disposition. I went over her several times for conformation and, to this day, cannot see why she could not finish in the show ring. She was sound and had a beautiful layback of shoulder, something sadly lacking in many of this breed that are shown but not coursed. This is a breed that should be allowed to do something that they would thoroughly enjoy.

OFFICIAL STANDARD FOR THE AFGHAN HOUND

General Appearance—The Afghan Hound is an aristocrat, his whole appearance one of dignity and aloofness with no trace of plainness or coarseness. He has a straight front, proudly carried head, eyes gazing into the distance as if in memory of ages past. The striking characteristics of the breed—exotic, or "Eastern," expression, long silky topknot, peculiar coat pattern, very prominent hipbones, large feet, and the impression of a somewhat exaggerated bend in the stifle due to profuse trouserings—stand out clearly, giving the Afghan Hound the appearance of what he is, a king of dogs, that has held true to tradition throughout the ages.

Head—The head is of good length, showing much refinement, the skull evenly balanced with the foreface. There is a slight prominence of the nasal bone structure causing a slightly Roman appearance, the center line running up over the foreface with little or no stop, falling away in front of the eyes so there is an absolutely clear outlook with no interference; the underjaw showing great strength, the jaws long and punishing; the mouth level, meaning that the teeth from the upper jaw and lower jaw match evenly, neither overshot nor undershot. This is a difficult mouth to breed. A scissors bite is even more punishing and can be more easily bred into a dog than a level mouth, and a

Afghans gathering for inspection before a course.

Going to the line.

On the lure.

dog having a scissors bite, where the lower teeth slip inside and rest against the teeth of the upper jaw, should not be penalized. The occipital bone is very prominent. The head is surmounted by a topknot of long silky hair. *Ears*—The ears are long, set approximately on level with outer corners of the eyes, the leather of the ear reaching nearly to the end of the dog's nose, and covered with long silky hair. *Eyes*—The eyes are almond-shaped (almost triangular), never full or bulgy, and are dark in color. *Nose*—Nose is of good size, black in color. *Faults*—Coarseness; snipiness; overshot or undershot; eyes round or bulgy or light in color; exaggerated Roman nose; head not surmounted with topknot.

Neck—The neck is of good length, strong and arched, running in a curve to the shoulders, which are long and sloping and well laid back. *Faults*—Neck too short or too thick; a ewe neck; a goose neck; a neck lacking in substance.

Body—The back line appearing practically level from the shoulders to the loin. Strong and powerful and slightly arched, falling away toward the stern, with the hipbones very pronounced; well ribbed and tucked up in flanks. The height at the shoulders equals the distance from the chest to the buttocks; the brisket is well let down and of medium width. *Faults*—Roach back, sway-back, goose rump, slack loin; lack of prominence of hipbones; too much width of brisket, causing interference with elbows.

Tail—Tail set not too high on the body, having a ring, or a curve on the end, should never be curled over, or rest on the back, or be carried sideways; should never be bushy.

Legs—Forelegs are straight and strong, with great length between elbow and pastern; elbows well held in; forefeet large in both length and width; toes well arched; feet covered with long thick hair; fine in texture; pasterns long and straight; pads of feet unusually large and well down on the ground. Shoulders have plenty of angulation so that the legs are well set underneath the dog. Too much straightness of shoulder causes the dog to break down in the pasterns, and this is a serious fault. All four feet of the Afghan hound are in line with the body, turning neither in nor out. The hind feet are broad and of good length; the toes arched and covered with long thick hair; hindquarters powerful and well muscled, with great length between hip and hock; hocks are well let down; good angulation of both stifle and hock; slightly bowed from hock to crotch. *Faults*—Front or back feet thrown outward or inward; pads of feet not thick enough; or feet too small; or any other evidence of weakness in feet; weak or broken down pasterns; too straight in stifle; too long in hock.

Coat—Hindquarters, flanks, ribs, forequarters, and legs well covered with thick, silky hair, very fine in texture; ears and all four feet well feathered;

The Basenji differs sharply from the more typical sighthounds and tends to run a little slower than the others, but is good at following the lure and is in all respects an ardent hunter of great determination.

The barkless hounds of Africa lining up for inspection.

from in front of the shoulders, and also backwards from the shoulders along the saddle from the flanks and the ribs upwards, the hair is short and close, forming a smooth back in mature dogs—this is a traditional characteristic of the Afghan hound. The Afghan hound should be shown in its natural state; the coat is not clipped or trimmed; the head is surmounted (in the full sense of the word) with a topknot of long, silky hair—that is also an outstanding characteristic of the Afghan Hound. Showing of short hair on cuffs on either front or back legs is permissible. *Fault*—Lack of shorthaired saddle in mature dogs.

Height—Dogs, 27 inches, plus or minus one inch; bitches, 25 inches, plus or minus one inch.

Weight—Dogs, about 60 pounds; bitches, about 50 pounds.

Color—All colors are permissible, but color or color combinations are pleasing; white markings, especially on the head, are undesirable.

Gait—When running free, the Afghan hound moves at a gallop, showing great elasticity and spring in his smooth, powerful stride. When on a loose lead, the Afghan can trot at a fast pace; stepping along, he has the appearance of placing the hind feet directly in the footprints of the front feet, both thrown straight ahead. Moving with head and tail high, the whole appearance of the Afghan hound is one of great style and beauty.

Temperament—Aloof and dignified, yet gay. *Faults*—Sharpness or shyness.

Approved September 14, 1948

THE BASENJI

The Basenji, the smallest of all the coursing breeds, was admitted as a "sighthound" by the ASFA in 1979. Historically, it ranks up with some of the really ancient hounds. The Pharaohs of Egypt had packs of Basenjis, and they were also used for hunting by tribes in the Congo. They are versatile hounds and hunt by scent as well as by sight. In fact, due to their small size, they tend to use their noses more than their sight. In Africa, they are still used to drive various small game into nets that have been set out by hunters. They are best known as the "barkless" breed, having a rather shrill scream or whine rather than a bark.

In coursing, due to their small size and rather short legs, they are slower than almost any of the other sighthound breeds. This makes it easier for the lure operator when they are running within their breed but very difficult when they are running with the faster breeds for Best in Field. The Basenji tends to be feistier than the average sighthound, and I have seen some royal donnybrooks when three of them finish a course together. They do tend to follow the lure better than some of the other breeds, however, and seem to have excellent endurance. If a course has high and low places and the lure operator is not careful, these dogs can unsight quite easily due to their small size. Although they are recognized as sighthounds, in my opinion they are more scent- than sight-motivated but interesting to watch run.

OFFICIAL STANDARD FOR THE BASENJI

General Appearance—The Basenji is a small, short-haired hunting dog from Africa. It is short-backed and lightly built, appearing high on the leg compared to its length. The wrinkled head is proudly carried on a well-arched neck and the tail is set high and curled. Elegant and graceful, the whole demeanor is one of poise and inquiring alertness. The balanced structure and the smooth musculature enables it to move with ease and agility. The Basenji hunts by both sight and scent. *Characteristics*—The Basenji should not bark but is not mute. The wrinkled forehead, tightly curled tail and swift, effortless gait (resembling a racehorse trotting full out) are typical of the breed. *Faults*—Any departure from the following points must be considered a fault, and the seriousness with which the fault is regarded is to be in exact proportion to its degree.

Size, Proportion, Substance—Ideal height for dogs is 17 inches and bitches 16 inches. Dogs 17 inches and bitches 16 inches from front of chest to point of buttocks. Approximate weight for dogs, 24 pounds and bitches, 22 pounds. Lightly built within this height to weight ratio.

Head—The head is proudly carried. *Eyes*—Dark hazel to dark brown, almond shaped, obliquely set and farseeing, rims dark. *Ears*—Small, erect and slightly hooded, of fine texture and set well forward on top of head. The skull is flat, well chiseled and of medium width, tapering toward the eyes. The foreface tapers from eye to muzzle with a perceptible stop. Muzzle shorter than skull, neither coarse nor snipy, but with rounded cushions. Wrinkles appear upon the forehead when ears are erect, and are fine and profuse. Side wrinkles are desirable, but should never be exaggerated into dewlap. Wrinkles are most noticeable in puppies, and because of lack of shadowing, less noticeable in blacks, tricolors and brindles. *Nose*—Black greatly desired. *Teeth*—Evenly aligned with a scissors bite.

Neck, Topline, Body—Neck of good length, well crested and slightly full at base of throat. Well set into shoulders. *Topline*—Back level. *Body*—Balanced with a short back, short coupled and ending in a definite waist. Ribs moderately sprung, deep to elbows and oval. Slight forechest in front of point of shoulder. Chest of medium width. *Tail* is set high on topline, bends acutely forward and lies well curled over to either side.

Forequarters—Shoulders moderately laid back. Shoulder blade and upper arm of approximately equal length. Elbows tucked firmly against brisket. Legs straight with clean fine bone, long forearm and well-defined sinews. Pasterns of good length, strong and flexible. *Feet*—Small, oval and compact with thick pads and well arched toes. Dewclaws are usually removed.

Hindquarters—Medium width, strong and muscular, hocks well let down and turned neither in nor out, with long second thighs and moderately bent stifles. *Feet*—Same as in ''Forequarters.''

Coat and Color—Coat short and fine. Skin very pliant. *Color*—Chestnut red; pure black; tricolor (pure black and chestnut red); or brindle (black stripes on a background of chestnut red); all with white feet, chest and tail tip. White legs, blaze and collar optional. The amount of white should never predominate over primary color. Color and markings should be rich, clear and well-defined, with a distinct line of demarcation between the black and red of tricolors and the stripes of brindles.

Gait—Swift, tireless trot. Stride is long, smooth, effortless and the topline remains level. Coming and going, the straight column of bones from shoulder joint to foot and from hip joint to pad remains unbroken, converging toward the centerline under the body. The faster the trot, the greater the convergence.

Temperament—An intelligent, independent, but affectionate and alert breed. Can be aloof with strangers.

Approved May 8, 1990

THE BORZOI

In the United States before 1936, the Borzoi was known as the Russian Wolfhound, and it is still known by that name in several countries of the world. It does not date back as far as some other sighthounds, but we know that it dates from the time of Genghis Khan (around the thirteenth century) because hounds fitting the Borzoi's description were mentioned as the principal coursing dogs at that time.

Jumping to the present day, the Borzoi was one of the first hounds to be used in both open coursing and lure coursing because Lyle Gillette, the father of both sports, was an ardent Borzoi breeder. The parent Borzoi club was also always very interested in any type of fieldwork for the breed and therefore offered constant encouragement. From the first days of lure coursing, the Borzoi was known to hunt the lure rather than to chase it. Therefore many of the breed learned to "cut" during the course to try and catch the lure. I have seen very few experienced Borzois that exhibited any real urge to follow but many that were real headaches to lure operators. They are, however, thrilling to watch when they run a course. Although on the whole they are not as fast as some other sighthounds, they can turn on a quick burst of speed.

OFFICIAL STANDARD FOR THE BORZOI

General Appearance—The Borzoi was originally bred for the coursing of wild game on more or less open terrain, relying on sight rather than scent. To accomplish this purpose, the Borzoi needed particular structural qualities to chase, catch and hold his quarry. Special emphasis is placed on sound running gear, strong neck and jaws, courage and agility, combined with proper condition. The Borzoi should always possess unmistakable elegance, with flowing lines, graceful in motion or repose. Males, masculine without coarseness; bitches, feminine and refined.

Head—Skull slightly domed, long and narrow, with scarcely any perceptible stop, inclined to be Roman-nosed. Jaws long, powerful and deep, somewhat finer in bitches but not snipy. Teeth strong and clean with either an even or a scissors bite. Missing teeth should be penalized. Nose large and black.

Ears—Small and fine in quality, lying back on the neck when in repose with the tips when thrown back almost touching behind occiput; raised when at attention.

Eyes—Set somewhat obliquely, dark in color, intelligent but rather soft in expression; never round, full nor staring, nor light in color; eye rims dark; inner corner midway between tip of nose and occiput.

Neck—Clean, free from throatiness; slightly arched, very powerful and well set on.

The Borzoi is a hound of royal heritage and romantic legacy. A favorite sporting hound of imperial Russia, it has been used in the United States in open-field coursing, lure coursing and in actual hunting situations.

Borzois owned by Diana Darling make a memorable picture in full flight.

Shoulders—Sloping, fine at the withers and free from coarseness or lumber.

Chest—Rather narrow, with great depth of brisket.

Ribs—Only slightly sprung, but very deep, giving room for heart and lung play.

Back—Rising a little at the loins in a graceful curve.

Loins—Extremely muscular, but rather tucked up, owing to the great depth of chest and comparative shortness of back and ribs.

Forelegs—Bones straight and somewhat flattened like blades, with the narrower edge forward. The elbows have free play and are turned neither in nor out. Pasterns strong.

Feet—Hare-shaped, with well-arched knuckles, toes close and well padded.

Hindquarters—Long, very muscular and powerful with well bent stifles; somewhat wider than the forequarters; strong first and second thighs; hocks clean and well let down; legs parallel when viewed from the rear.

Dewclaws—Dewclaws, if any, on the hind legs are generally removed; dewclaws on the forelegs may be removed.

Tail—Long, set on and carried low in a graceful curve.

Coat—Long, silky (not woolly), either flat, wavy or rather curly. On the head, ears and front of legs it should be short and smooth; on the neck the frill should be profuse and rather curly. Feather on hindquarters and tail, long and profuse, less so on chest and back of forelegs.

Color—Any color, or combination of colors, is acceptable.

Size—Mature males should be at least 28 inches at the withers and mature bitches at least 26 inches at the withers. Dogs and bitches below these respective limits should be severely penalized; dogs and bitches above the respective limits should not be penalized as long as extra size is not acquired at the expense of symmetry, speed and staying quality. Range in weight for males from 75 to 105 pounds and for bitches from 15 to 20 pounds less.

Gait—Front legs must reach well out in front with pasterns strong and springy. Hackneyed motion with mincing gait is not desired nor is weaving and crossing. However, while the hind legs are wider apart than the front, the feet tend to move closer to the center line when the dog moves at a fast trot. When viewed from the side there should be a noticeable drive with a ground-covering stride from well-angulated stifles and hocks. The over-all appearance in motion should be that of effortless power, endurance, speed, agility, smoothness and grace.

The intensity is obvious.

The Greyhound, of ancient, honorable lineage, is the classic sighthound.

Chasing the "bunny."

The end of the chase.

The foregoing description is that of the ideal Borzoi. Any deviation from the above described dog must be penalized to the extent of the deviation, keeping in mind the importance of the contribution of the various features toward the basic original purpose of the breed.

Approved June 13, 1972

THE GREYHOUND

The Greyhound is one of the more ancient sighthound breeds, dating back to at least 3000 B.C. It has always been used as the English hare- or rabbit-coursing dog because the English terrain is eminently suited to its build. It is undoubtedly the fastest of all sighthound breeds, but some question its endurance and its quick-turning ability. It is even-tempered and gentle and really likes to run, a quality that shows on the coursing field. It still makes its mark in open coursing and is being used more and more in lure coursing. The reason for this is the National Greyhound Association (NGA) dog, which is bred exclusively for pari-mutuel racing. Until recently, if a so-called track Greyhound could not "cut the mustard" in racing, it was humanely destroyed. Then, about eight years ago, came a great surge of interest in saving these gentle souls and, before long, rescue groups appeared all over the country. As a result, people discovered what a marvelous pet an ex-track Greyhound can be. When they also found out that Greyhounds love to run the lure and can easily be taught the rudiments of lure coursing, there was a surge of this breed (and their owners) into the sport. I have run Greyhounds right off the track myself and can vouch for their great speed. Although they are only raced up to 400 yards, and some of them tend to fade in a long course, I believe that they are the coming breed in lure coursing.

OFFICIAL STANDARD FOR THE GREYHOUND

Head—Long and narrow, fairly wide between the ears, scarcely perceptible stop, little or no development of nasal sinuses, good length of muzzle, which should be powerful without coarseness. Teeth very strong and even in front.

Ears—Small and fine in texture, thrown back and folded, except when excited, when they are semipricked.

Eyes—Dark, bright, intelligent, indicating spirit.

Neck—Long, muscular, without throatiness, slightly arched, and widening gradually into the shoulder.

Shoulders—Placed as obliquely as possible, muscular without being loaded.

Forelegs—Perfectly straight, set well into the shoulders, neither turned in nor out, pasterns strong.

Chest—Deep, and as wide as consistent with speed, fairly well-sprung ribs.

Back—Muscular and broad.

Loins—Good depth of muscle, well arched, well cut up in the flanks.

Hindquarters—Long, very muscular and powerful, wide and well let-down, well-bent stifles. Hocks well bent and rather close to ground, wide but straight fore and aft.

Feet—Hard and close, rather more hare than cat-feet, well knuckled up with good strong claws.

Tail—Long, fine and tapering with a slight upward curve.

Coat—Short, smooth and firm in texture.

Color—Immaterial.

Weight—Dogs, 65 to 70 pounds; bitches, 60 to 65 pounds.

SCALE OF POINTS

General symmetry and quality	10	Back	10
Head and neck	20	Quarters	20
Chest and shoulders	20	Legs and feet	20
		TOTAL	100

THE IBIZAN HOUND

Although the Ibizan Hound dates back to about 3800 B.C., it is relatively new to both the show ring and to lure coursing. It was not recognized as a single breed by the AKC until 1976, and it entered lure coursing at about the same time. As its name implies, this breed came from the isle of Ibiza, part of the Balearic group in the Mediterranean off southern Spain. One of the breed's claims to fame is that it

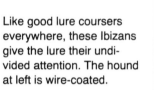

The Ibizan Hound, named for the island of Ibiza in the Balearics, is a relative newcomer to the American purebred scene. As hunting hounds they have many talents unusual among sighthounds and have a faithful following in the field and on the bench.

Like good lure coursers everywhere, these Ibizans give the lure their undivided attention. The hound at left is wire-coated.

Peter Parker with his AKC field champion Ibizan Hound, Smotare's Bramblewood Lizard.

was an Ibizan Hound that accompanied Hannibal across the Alps along with his elephants. In Ibiza they were known as an all-around hunting dog. While fanciers of other breeds have made this claim, I have done some hunting with an Ibizan and have seen them both point birds and flush them. The Ibizan has an excellent nose for a sighthound and tends to use it well, especially when rabbits dive into brushy cover. Another distinguishing feature of these hounds is that they give tongue both on line and while they are running. It makes for an exciting course although sometimes other contestants don't like it when their hounds are running for Best in Field. Ibizans are an amicable, gentle breed and tend to be clownish on occasion. There are both smooth and wire-coated individuals; the latter is a fascinating variation.

They reach a medium speed and do not have too much agility on the turns, but they have good follow and can run forever. A trio of Ibizans makes for a very spectacular coursing run.

OFFICIAL STANDARD FOR THE IBIZAN HOUND

General Appearance—The Ibizan's clean-cut lines, large prick ears and light pigment give it a unique appearance. A hunting dog whose quarry is primarily rabbits, this ancient hound was bred for thousands of years with function being of prime importance. Lithe and racy, the Ibizan possesses a deerlike elegance combined with the power of a hunter. Strong, without appearing heavily muscled, the Ibizan is a hound of moderation. With the exception of the ears, he should not appear extreme or exaggerated. In the field the Ibizan is as fast as top coursing breeds and without equal in agility, high jumping and broad jumping ability. He is able to spring to great heights from a standstill.

Size, Proportion, Substance—*Size*—The height of dogs is 23½ inches to 27½ inches at the withers. Bitches are 22½ to 26 inches at the withers. There is no preference for size within this range. Sizes slightly over or under the norms are not to be regarded as demerits when other qualities are good. *Weight*—Average weight of dogs is 50 pounds; bitches, 45 pounds. ***Proportion***—Slightly longer than tall. **Substance**—The Ibizan possesses clean, fine bone. The muscling is strong, yet flat, with no sign of heaviness.

Head—Long and narrow in the form of a sharp cone truncated at its base. Finely chiseled and extremely dry fleshed. *Expression*—The Ibizan has an elegant, deer-like look. The *eyes* are oblique and small, ranging in color from clear amber to caramel. The rims are the color of the nose and are fully or partially pigmented. The appearance of the eye is intelligent, alert and inquisitive. The *ears* are large, pointed, and natural. On alert the ear should never droop, bend or crease. Highly mobile, the ear can point forward, sideways, or be folded backward, according to mood. On alert, the lowest point of the base is at level of the eye. On frontal examination, the height of the ear is approximately 2½ times that of the widest point of the base. *Skull*—Long and flat, prominent occipital bone, little defined *stop*; narrow brow. The *muzzle* is elongated, fine, and slender with a very slight Roman convex. The length from the eyes to point of nose is equal to the distance from eyes to occiput. The muzzle and skull are on parallel *planes*. The *nose* is prominent, extending beyond the lower jaw. It is of a rosy flesh color, never black or liver, and tends to harmonize with the coat. Pigment is solid or butterfly. Nostrils are open. *Lips* are thin and tight and the color of the nose. Flews are tight and dry fleshed. *Bite*—The teeth are perfectly opposed in a scissors bite; strong and well set.

Neck, Topline, Body—The *neck* is long, slender, slightly arched and strong, yet flat muscled. The *topline*, from ears to tail, is smooth and flowing. The *back* is level and straight. *Body*—The chest is deep and long with the breast-bone sharply angled and prominent. The ribs are slightly sprung. The brisket is approximately 2½ inches above the elbow. The deepest part of the chest, behind the elbow, is nearly to or to the elbow. The abdomen is well tucked up, but not exaggerated. The *loin* is very slightly arched, of medium breadth and well muscled. The *croup* is very slightly sloping. The *tail* is set low, highly mobile, and reaches at least to the hock. It is carried in a sickle, ring, or saber position, according to the mood and individual specimen.

Forequarters—*Angulation* is moderate. The *shoulders* are elastic but never loose with moderate breadth at the withers. The shoulder blades are well laid back. At the *point of the shoulder* they join to a rather upright *upper arm*. The *elbow* is positioned in front of the deepest part of the chest. It is well held in but not so much as to restrict movement. *Legs*—The forearms are very long, strong, straight, and close, lying flat on the chest and continuing in a straight line to the ground. Bone is clean and fine. The *pasterns* are strong and flexible, slightly sloping, with well developed tendons. *Dewclaw* removal is optional. *Feet*: hare-foot. The toes are long, closed and very strong. Inter-digital spaces are well protected by hair. Pads are durable. Nails are white.

Hindquarters—*Angulation* is moderate with the hindquarters being set under the body. *Legs*—The thighs are very strong with flat muscling. The hocks are straight when viewed from the rear. Bone is clean and fine. There are no rear dewclaws. The *feet* are as in front.

Coat—There are two types of coat; both untrimmed. *Short*—shortest on head and ears and longest at back of the thighs and under the tail. *Wire-haired* can be from one to three inches in length with a possible generous moustache.

There is more hair on the back, back of thighs, and tail. Both types of coat are hard in texture and neither coat is preferable to the other.

Color—White or red (from light, yellowish-red called "lion" to deep red), solid or in any combination. No color or pattern is preferable to the other. *Disqualify* any color other than white or red.

Gait—An efficient, light and graceful single-tracking movement. A suspended trot with joint flexion when viewed from the side. The Ibizan exhibits smooth reach in front with balanced rear drive, giving the appearance of skimming over the ground.

Temperament—The Ibizan Hound is even-tempered, affectionate and loyal. Extremely versatile and trainable, he makes an excellent family pet, and is well suited to the breed ring, obedience, tracking and lure-coursing. He exhibits a keen, natural hunting instinct with much determination and stamina in the field.

DISQUALIFICATION

Any color other than white or red.

Approved September 11, 1989

THE IRISH WOLFHOUND

Although many claims have been made regarding the antiquity of the Irish Wolfhound, the modern hound does not hark back any further than around 1862. The breed had become almost extinct at that time when Captain George A. Graham, a Scotsman and British army veteran, revived it. From all that I have read, he had a few remnants of Irish hounds and a few Scottish Deerhounds and he interbred them, using the larger and bigger-boned animals to create the present-day version of this time-honored giant.

Many of the present-day "show"' Irish Wolfhounds have been bred purely for size, and they are too ungainly to really run. The few fast Irish Wolfhounds are smaller than the average show specimens. It's too bad that lure coursing started formally only in 1972. I knew many Wolfhounds bred by Alma Starbuck in the 1950s that would have been fully capable of running the lure as well as showing in conformation. What happened to the stamina and life span of this breed is a mystery. Caring breeders should do whatever is needed to restore

The Irish Wolfhound, awesome by any standard, is yet another breed with a long, romantic history. The breed is not often seen in lure coursing, but some hounds have proven equal to the challenge.

A pair of Irish Wolfhounds, owned by Judy Wozniak, breezing through the snow.

the breed's ancient glory. A few kennels still breed good coursing hounds and to them full marks.

Irish Wolfhounds are slower than most other sighthound breeds and often find it difficult to negotiate the turns of a course. They are, however, amiable dogs with easygoing dispositions. In addition, the few that are seen in lure coursing do an excellent job and corral more than their share of Bests in Field. I have spent considerable time trying to persuade some of my friends who show Irish Wolfhounds to try them in the field, but it seems to be a lost cause.

OFFICIAL STANDARD FOR THE IRISH WOLFHOUND

General Appearance—Of great size and commanding appearance, the Irish Wolfhound is remarkable in combining power and swiftness with keen sight. The largest and tallest of the galloping hounds, in general type he is a rough-coated, Greyhoundlike breed; very muscular, strong though gracefully built; movements easy and active; head and neck carried high, the tail carried with an upward sweep with a slight curve towards the extremity. The minimum height and weight of dogs should be 32 inches and 120 pounds; of bitches, 30 inches and 105 pounds; these to apply only to hounds over 18 months of age. Anything below this should be debarred from competition. Great size, including height at shoulder and proportionate length of body, is the desideratum to be aimed at, and it is desired to firmly establish a race that shall average from 32 to 34 inches in dogs, showing the requisite power, activity, courage and symmetry.

Head—Long, the frontal bones of the forehead very slightly raised and very little indentation between the eyes. Skull, not too broad. Muzzle, long and moderately pointed. Ears, small and Greyhoundlike in carriage.

Neck—Rather long, very strong and muscular, well arched, without dewlap or loose skin about the throat.

Chest—Very deep. Breast, wide.

Back—Rather long than short. Loins arched.

Tail—Long and slightly curved, of moderate thickness, and well covered with hair.

Belly—Well drawn up.

Forequarters—Shoulders, muscular, giving breadth of chest, set sloping. Elbows well under, neither turned inwards nor outwards.

Leg—Forearm muscular, and the whole leg strong and quite straight.

Hindquarters—Muscular thighs and second thigh long and strong as in the Greyhound, and hocks well let down and turning neither in nor out.

Feet—Moderately large and round, neither turned inwards nor outwards. Toes, well arched and closed. Nails, very strong and curved.

Hair—Rough and hard on body, legs and head; especially wiry and long over eyes and underjaw.

Color and Markings—The recognized colors are gray, brindle, red, black, pure white, fawn, or any other color that appears in the Deerhound.

FAULTS

Too light or heavy a head, too highly arched frontal bone; large ears and hanging flat to the face; short neck; full dewlap; too narrow or too broad a chest; sunken or hollow or quite straight back; bent forelegs; overbent fetlocks; twisted feet; spreading toes; too curly a tail; weak hindquarters and a general want of muscle; too short in body. Lips or nose liver-colored or lacking pigmentation.

LIST OF POINTS IN ORDER OF MERIT

1. *Typical.* The Irish Wolfhound is a rough-coated Greyhoundlike breed, the tallest of the coursing hounds and remarkable in combining power and swiftness.
2. *Great size* and commanding appearance.
3. Movements easy and active.
4. Head, long and level, carried high.
5. Forelegs, heavily boned, quite straight; elbows well set under.
6. Thighs long and muscular; second thighs, well muscled, stifles nicely bent.
7. Coat, rough and hard, specially wiry and long over eyes and under jaw.
8. Body, long, well ribbed up, with ribs well sprung, and great breadth across hips.
9. Loins arched, belly well drawn up.
10. Ears, small, with Greyhoundlike carriage.
11. Feet, moderately large and round; toes, close, well arched.
12. Neck, long, well arched and very strong.
13. Chest, very deep, moderately broad.
14. Shoulders, muscular, set sloping.
15. Tail, long and slightly curved.
16. Eyes, dark.

The Pharaoh Hound is an ancient breed that was brought to the island of Malta more than two thousand years ago. Its uncanny similarity to hounds depicted in Egyptian hieroglyphics during the reign of the Pharaohs is yet another indicator of its great antiquity.

Ch. Kamaraj Scirocco, LCM 3, taking a turn with style. Owner, Marilyn Smith.

Note—The above in no way alters the "Standard of Excellence," which must in all cases be rigidly adhered to; they simply give the various points in order of merit. If in any case they appear at variance with Standard of Excellence, it is the latter which is correct.

Approved September 12, 1950

THE PHARAOH HOUND

The Pharaoh Hound is one of an elite group of really ancient sighthounds dating back at least as far as 3000 B.C. They were brought to the island of Malta well before the birth of Christ and were used there mainly to hunt rabbit and warn farmers of unwanted trespassers on their property. So highly was this breed regarded that in 1979 it was declared the National Dog of Malta and a commemorative medal bearing the likeness of a standing Pharaoh was minted in its honor.

In 1977, the ASFA recognized the Pharaoh Hound as a sighthound and allowed Pharaohs to run in their sanctioned lure-coursing trials. It wasn't until 1984, however, that the AKC recognized the Pharaoh as a single breed, including it in the Hound Group.

The Pharaoh is a self-colored red dog. One of its distinguishing features is the distinctly bright-red blush that envelops its face when it becomes excited, and, believe me, when it sees the lure it becomes excited. It is also quite noisy on line and usually gives tongue all the way around the course. You don't have to be watching to know the Pharaohs are going on line. Your ears will convey the message clearly. This breed tends to be a bit standoffish with strangers. With those they know, however, they are very friendly. They are very fast but sometimes tend to run all over the field rather than chase the lure. One of the best known lure-coursing Pharaohs has a name that ends in "shut-up."

OFFICIAL STANDARD FOR THE PHARAOH HOUND

General Appearance—General Appearance is one of grace, power and speed. The Pharaoh Hound is medium sized, of noble bearing with hard clean-cut lines—graceful, well balanced, very fast with free easy movement and alert expression.

The following description is that of the ideal Pharaoh Hound. Any deviation from the below described dog must be penalized to the extent of the deviation.

Size, Proportion, Substance—*Height*—Dogs 23 inches–25 inches. Bitches 21 inches–24 inches. Allover balance must be maintained. Length of body from breast to haunch bone slightly longer than height of withers to ground. Lithe.

Head—Alert *expression*. *Eyes* amber colored, blending with coat; oval, moderately deep set with keen intelligent expression. *Ears* medium high set, carried erect when alert, but very mobile, broad at the base, fine and large. *Skull* long, lean and chiseled. Only slight stop. Foreface slightly longer than the skull. Top of the skull parallel with the foreface representing a blunt wedge. *Nose* flesh colored, blending with the coat. No other color. Powerful jaws with strong teeth. Scissors *bite*.

Neck, Topline, Body—*Neck* long, lean and muscular with a slight arch to carry the head on high. Clean throat line. Almost straight *topline*. Slight slope from croup to root of tail. *Body* lithe. Deep brisket almost down to point of elbow. Ribs well sprung. Moderate tuck-up. *Tail* medium set—fairly thick at the base and tapering whiplike, reaching below the point of hock in repose. Well carried and curved when in action. The tail should not be tucked between the legs. A screw tail is a fault.

Forequarters—*Shoulders* long and sloping and well laid back. Strong without being loaded. *Elbows* well tucked in. *Forelegs* straight and parallel. Pasterns strong. Dewclaws may be removed. *Feet* neither cat nor hare but strong, well knuckled and firm, turning neither in nor out. Paws well padded.

Hindquarters—Strong and muscular. Limbs parallel. Moderate sweep of stifle. Well developed second thigh. Dewclaws may be removed. *Feet* as in front.

Coat—Short and glossy, ranging from fine and close to slightly harsh with no feathering. Accident blemishes should not be considered as faults.

Color—Ranging from tan/rich tan/chestnut with white markings allowed as follows: White tip on tail strongly desired. White on chest (called ''the Star''). White on toes and slim white snip on center line of face permissible. Flecking or other white undesirable, except for any solid white spot on the back of neck, shoulder, or any part of the back or sides of the dog, which is a *disqualification*.

Gait—Free and flowing; the head should be held fairly high and the dog should cover the ground well without any apparent effort. The legs and feet should move in line with the body; any tendency to throw the feet sideways, or a high stepping "hackney" action is a definite fault.

Temperament—Intelligent, friendly, affectionate and playful. Alert and active. Very fast with a marked keenness for hunting, both by sight and scent.

Any solid white spot on the back of neck, shoulder, or any part of the back or sides of the dog.

Approved May 10, 1983
Reformatted April 3, 1989

THE RHODESIAN RIDGEBACK

The Rhodesian Ridgeback is the newest member of the coursing fraternity of sighthounds. For the past several years the ASFA had the Ridgeback on a provisional status, and in April 1993 accorded it full status. On September 1, 1992, the AKC admitted the breed and gave it full status in its coursing trial format.

I happen to have been present at the first three AKC trials in which the Rhodesian Ridgeback competed, and a large group was entered. The AKC runs tests for Junior Courser (JC), and in these tests the dogs run singly and have to run twice on different days under different judges before they can have the JC title and run in the open stake. Some of the Ridgebacks entered made it, others did not; but it was a good beginning.

The Ridgeback evolved sometime after 1707, when immigration to South Africa was closed. The breeds living there at the time—the Great Dane, the Mastiff, the Greyhound and the Bloodhound—all played a part in developing the Ridgeback. The Hottentots, a native South African tribe, kept a semiwild hunting dog distinguished by a ridge of hair growing against the grain on its back. This dog obviously also played a big part in the development of the Ridgeback. Only time will tell if the Rhodesian Ridgeback will make it as a true coursing dog.

The Rhodesian Ridgeback was developed by European settlers in South Africa in response to their need for a capable farm/hunting/guard dog. Although it is distinctly different from classic sighthounds, it does have Greyhound influence and does have a good following in modern lure coursing.

A group of Ridgebacks and their supporters at the first AKC trial they were admitted to. The date was September 1, 1992. Also present were Dean Wright, AKC Coursing Director (extreme left), and Robert McKowen, AKC Vice President of Performance Events (third from right).

A Rhodesian field off and running.

OFFICIAL STANDARD FOR THE RHODESIAN RIDGEBACK

The peculiarity of this breed is the *ridge* on the back, which is formed by the hair growing in the opposite direction to the rest of the coat. The ridge must be regarded as the characteristic feature of the breed. The ridge should be clearly defined, tapering and symmetrical. It should start immediately behind the shoulders and continue to a point between the prominence of the hips, and should contain two identical crowns opposite each other. The lower edges of the crown should not extend further down the ridge than one third of the ridge.

General Appearance—The Ridgebacks should represent a strong muscular and active dog, symmetrical in outline, and capable of great endurance with a fair amount of speed.

Head—Should be of a fair length, the skull flat and rather broad between the ears and should be free from wrinkles when in repose. The stop should be reasonably well defined. *Muzzle*—Should be long, deep and powerful, jaws level and strong with well-developed teeth, especially the canines or holders. The lips clean, closely fitting the jaws. *Eyes*—Should be moderately well apart, and should be round, bright and sparkling, with intelligent expression, their color harmonizing with the color of the dog. *Ears*—Should be set rather high, of medium size, rather wide at base, and tapering to a rounded point. They should be carried close to the head. *Nose*—Should be black, or brown, in keeping with the color of the dog. No other colored nose is permissible. A black nose should be accompanied by dark eyes, a brown nose by amber eyes.

Neck and Shoulders—The neck should be fairly strong and free from throatiness. The shoulders should be sloping, clean and muscular, denoting speed.

Body, Back, Chest and Loins—The chest should not be too wide, but very deep and capacious; ribs moderately well sprung, never rounded like barrel hoops (which would indicate want of speed), the back powerful, the loins strong, muscular and slightly arched.

Legs and Feet—The forelegs should be perfectly straight, strong and heavy in bone; elbows close to the body. The feet should be compact, with well-arched toes, round, tough, elastic pads, protected by hair between the toes and pads. In the hind legs the muscles should be clean, well defined, and hocks well down.

Tail—Should be strong at the insertion, and generally tapering towards the end, free from coarseness. It should not be inserted too high or too low, and should be carried with a slight curve upwards, never curled.

Coat—Should be short and dense, sleek and glossy in appearance, but neither woolly nor silky.

The Saluki is believed to be the world's oldest known dog breed. A hunting hound of great ability, it has been held in the highest esteem in the Islamic culture, which generally considers other dogs "unclean." The breed still demonstrates its talent in the field, given the proper opportunity.

Ch. Solari Sa Shahir Saamira, F. Ch., won the Pyramid Cup at the 1992 Saluki Club of America Specialty.
Alverson

Arthur Beaman with a father-and-son pair of Saluki speedsters.

Color—Light wheaten to red wheaten. A little white on the chest and toes permissible but excessive white there and any white on the belly or above the toes is undesirable.

Size—A mature Ridgeback should be a handsome, upstanding dog; dogs should be of a height of 25 to 27 inches, and bitches 24 to 26 inches.

Weight—(Desirable) dogs 75 pounds, bitches 65 pounds.

SCALE OF POINTS

Ridge	20	Coat	5
Head	15	Tail	5
Neck and shoulders	10	Size, symmetry, general	
Body, back, chest, loins	10	appearance	20
Legs and feet	15	TOTAL	100

Approved November, 1955

THE SALUKI

You'll have to forgive me if I take a bit more space with the Saluki than with some of the other breeds. I have been owned by this breed for the past fourteen years, and I still can't figure them out. I wanted a breed that didn't have to be trained. Believe me, I found one!

According to everything I have read, the Saluki is the oldest domesticated dog known to man. Dating back to 7000 B.C., Salukis have been used on almost all types of game, and I believe they are the forebears of many of our present-day hunting breeds. According to my Cambridge Encyclopedia, the Saluki is also the fastest dog in the world, attaining speeds of forty-one to forty-five miles per hour. I can vouch personally for their endurance as I have had to chase my hounds for up to three miles trying to catch them after a course had been run. The Saluki is a completely independent hound: You do things their way or it doesn't get done. On the other hand, they are tremendous athletes.

The heavy feathering on their feet and toes (when show handlers don't trim it off) renders them impervious to almost any type of terrain. They have tremendous speed and excellent turning ability. Many learn to cut the course, or cheat, at an early age, but when you get one that

Salukis on the line.

Ch. Solari Sa Baahir, F. Ch., at full gallop.

wants to follow, it takes a good lure operator to keep the lure ahead of your hound. They are both a pleasure and a horror to course. A large, securely fenced-in area, plus a good strong leash and collar, are all imperative if one is to keep these dogs. The Saluki is a long-lived breed, capable of attaining an age of sixteen or more. Most, however, are killed by cars at an early age. They don't chase cars; they race them. I have an eleven-year-old who still loves to chase the lure or anything else that moves.

Comparatively few Salukis course because their owners are afraid to let them off leash. Almost all the people who course their Salukis also show them, but a bare 20 percent of the show people course their dogs. Salukis are usually aloof with people and show their emotions only when they are brought up to line. Then, if you watch their eyes, you'll see the happiness.

I have dealt with purebred dogs for over forty-five years, and have owned many good show dogs and field dogs, but no breed has given me as many thrills or disappointments as the oldest one of all—the Saluki.

OFFICIAL STANDARD FOR THE SALUKI

Head—Long and narrow, skull moderately wide between the ears, not domed, stop not pronounced, the whole showing great quality. Nose black or liver. *Ears*—Long and covered with long silky hair hanging close to the skull and mobile. *Eyes*—Dark to hazel and bright; large and oval, but not prominent. *Teeth*—Strong and level.

Neck—Long, supple and well muscled.

Chest—Deep and moderately narrow.

Forequarters—Shoulders sloping and set well back, well muscled without being coarse. *Forelegs*—Straight and long from the elbow to the knee.

Hindquarters—Strong, hipbones set well apart and stifle moderately bent, hocks low to the ground, showing galloping and jumping power.

Loin and Back—Back fairly broad, muscles slightly arched over loin.

Feet—Of moderate length, toes long and well arched, not splayed out, but at the same time not cat-footed; the whole being strong and supple and well feathered between the toes.

Tail—Long, set on low and carried naturally in a curve, well feathered on the underside with long silky hair, not bushy.

The Scottish Deerhound, true to its ancient heritage, is equally capable in open-field coursing and lure coursing.

Many Deerhounds, such as these, can behave calmly on the line . . .

. . . but they know what "Tally-Ho" means.

Coat—Smooth and of a soft silky texture, slight feather on the legs, feather at the back of the thighs and sometimes with slight woolly feather on the thigh and shoulder.

Colors—White, cream, fawn, golden, red, grizzle and tan, tricolor (white, black and tan) and black and tan.

General Appearance—The whole appearance of this breed should give an impression of grace and symmetry and of great speed and endurance coupled with strength and activity to enable it to kill gazelle or other quarry over deep sand or rocky mountains. The expression should be dignified and gentle with deep, faithful, far-seeing eyes. Dogs should average in height from 23 to 28 inches and bitches may be considerably smaller, this being very typical of the breed.

The Smooth Variety—In this variety the points should be the same with the exception of the coat, which has no feathering.

THE SCOTTISH DEERHOUND

As I mentioned in the Preface, the Scottish Deerhound was the first purebred dog I owned. Although there are many theories about their antiquity, they were definitely used in the Highlands of Scotland to bring down the large Scottish red stag, which often weighed more than 300 pounds. Those were the days of muzzle-loading guns with one shot only, and many deer were wounded. When that happened, a leash of three Deerhounds was let loose to drive the deer to bay and hold it until the hunter could arrive to administer the coup de grace. There is no doubt in my mind that the same Captain Graham I mentioned in the Irish Wolfhound section also increased the Deerhound population while he was bringing back the Wolfhound. During World War II there was little food for Deerhounds in England, and so a number were shipped to Mrs. Anna H. Huntington and her Stanerigg Kennels in Connecticut. This also helped to preserve the breed.

The Deerhound was an excellent open coursing dog and a fair number are competing quite successfully in present-day lure coursing trials. The coursers tend to be smaller in size than those shown on the bench. You can usually tell a good running Deerhound from the way it reacts to the lure. It stiffens, and its eyes become glued to the lure. Some of the larger specimens are so relaxed they often won't pay any attention to the lure unless they are teased.

OFFICIAL STANDARD FOR THE SCOTTISH DEERHOUND

Head—Should be broadest at the ears, narrowing slightly to the eyes, with the muzzle tapering more decidedly to the nose. The muzzle should be pointed, but the teeth and lips level. The head should be long, the skull flat rather than round with a very slight rise over the eyes but nothing approaching a stop. The hair on the skull should be moderately long and softer than the rest of the coat. The nose should be black (in some blue fawns—blue) and slightly aquiline. In lighter colored dogs the black muzzle is preferable. There should be a good mustache of rather silky hair and a fair beard.

Ears—Should be set on high; in repose, folded back like a Greyhound's, though raised above the head in excitement without losing the fold, and even in some cases semierect. A prick ear is bad. Big thick ears hanging flat to the head or heavily coated with long hair are bad faults. The ears should be soft, glossy, like a mouse's coat to the touch and the smaller the better. There should be no long coat or long fringe, but there is sometimes a silky, silvery coat on the body of the ear and the tip. On all Deerhounds, irrespective of color of coat, the ears should be black or dark colored.

Neck and Shoulders—The neck should be long—of a length befitting the Greyhound character of the dog. Extreme length is neither necessary nor desirable. Deerhounds do not stoop to their work like the Greyhounds. The mane, which every good specimen should have, sometimes detracts from the apparent length of the neck. The neck, however, must be strong as is necessary to hold a stag. The nape of the neck should be very prominent where the head is set on, and the throat clean cut at the angle and prominent. Shoulders should be well sloped; blades well back and not too much width between them. Loaded and straight shoulders are very bad faults.

Tail—Should be tolerably long, tapering and reaching to within 1½ inches of the ground and about 1½ inches below the hocks. Dropped perfectly down or curved when the Deerhound is still, when in motion or excited, curved, but in no instance lifted out of line of the back. It should be well covered with hair, on the inside, thick and wiry, underside longer and towards the end a slight fringe is not objectionable. A curl or ring tail is undesirable.

Eyes—Should be dark—generally dark brown, brown or hazel. A very light eye is not liked. The eye should be moderately full, with a soft look in repose, but a keen, far-away look when the Deerhound is roused. Rims of eyelids should be black.

Body—General conformation is that of a Greyhound of larger size and bone. Chest deep rather than broad but not too narrow or slab-sided. Good girth of chest is indicative of great lung power. The loin well arched and drooping to the tail. A straight back is not desirable, this formation being unsuited for uphill work, and very unsightly.

Legs and Feet—Legs should be broad and flat, and good broad forearms and elbows are desirable. Forelegs must, of course, be as straight as possible. Feet close and compact, with well-arranged toes. The hindquarters drooping, and as broad and powerful as possible, the hips being set wide apart. A narrow rear denotes lack of power. The stifles should be well bent, with great length from hip to hock, which should be broad and flat. Cowhocks, weak pasterns, straight stifles and splay feet are very bad faults.

Coat—The hair on the body, neck and quarters should be harsh and wiry, about 3 or 4 inches long; that on the head, breast and belly much softer. There should be a slight fringe on the inside of the forelegs and hind legs but nothing approaching the "feather" of a Collie. A woolly coat is bad. Some good strains have a mixture of silky coat with the hard which is preferable to a woolly coat. The climate of the United States tends to produce the mixed coat. The ideal coat is a thick, close-lying ragged coat, harsh or crisp to the touch.

Color—is a matter of fancy, but the dark blue-gray is most preferred. Next come the darker and lighter grays or brindles, the darkest being generally preferred. Yellow and sandy red or red fawn, especially with black ears and muzzles, are equally high in estimation. This was the color of the oldest known strains—the McNeil and Chesthill Menzies. White is condemned by all authorities, but a white chest and white toes, occurring as they do in many of the darkest-colored dogs, are not objected to, although the less the better, for the Deerhound is a self-colored dog. A white blaze on the head, or a white collar, should entirely disqualify. The less white the better but a slight white tip to the stern occurs in some of the best strains.

Height—*Height of Dogs*—From 30 to 32 inches, or even more if there be symmetry without coarseness, which is rare.

Height of Bitches—From 28 inches upwards. There is no objection to a bitch being large, unless too coarse, as even at her greatest height she does not approach that of the dog, and therefore could not be too big for work as overbig dogs are.

Weight—From 85 to 110 pounds in dogs, and from 75 to 95 pounds in bitches.

POINTS OF THE DEERHOUND
ARRANGED IN ORDER OF IMPORTANCE

1. *Typical*—A Deerhound should resemble a rough-coated Greyhound of larger size and bone.

2. *Movements*—Easy, active and true.
3. As tall as possible consistent with quality.
4. *Head*—Long, level, well balanced, carried high.
5. *Body*—Long, very deep in brisket, well-sprung ribs and great breadth across hips.
6. *Forelegs*—Strong and quite straight, with elbows neither in nor out.
7. *Thighs*—Long and muscular, second thighs well muscled, stifles well bent.
8. *Loins*—Well arched, and belly well drawn up.
9. *Coat*—Rough and hard, with softer beard and brows.
10. *Feet*—Close, compact, with well-knuckled toes.
11. *Ears*—Small (dark) with Greyhoundlike carriage.
12. *Eyes*—Dark, moderately full.
13. *Neck*—Long, well arched, very strong with prominent nape.
14. *Shoulders*—Clean, set sloping.
15. *Chest*—Very deep but not too narrow.
16. *Tail*—Long and curved slightly, carried low.
17. *Teeth*—Strong and level.
18. *Nails*—Strong and curved.

DISQUALIFICATION

White blaze on the head, or a white collar.

Approved March, 1935

THE WHIPPET

It has often been said that without the Whippet, there would be little lure coursing. At any rate, without this breed lure coursing trials would be much smaller and some of the clubs would not exist. It is the second smallest of the sighthound group, but it has lots of fire and speed. This is probably because the breed was created by crossing small Greyhounds with one or more terrier breeds. The Whippet has been used a great deal for racing in England as well as for coursing and, consequently, has been considered the "poor man's" racehorse. A Whippet that is bred to run will usually chase a lure even when it knows the lure is artificial, but not always. I know a Whippet whose kennel mate is a field champion who couldn't care less about lures. But when the two are running loose in the field, it is the Whippet that

The Whippet is very popular in lure coursing and represents a large portion of the hounds in competition. The breed has courage, ability and desire, and is often a source of some very exciting moments in a course.

Ch. Bitterblue's Raybar Peyote, owned by Linda Garwacki, flying for the fun of it.
Jenny Philips

Lure-coursing meets are ideal places to socialize puppies destined to become future runners and show dogs. These young Whippets are learning that gatherings of people and hounds can be a special kind of fun.

will *not* chase lures that will corner and kill almost any type of small game—woodchuck, possum, even raccoons and, of course, an occasional rabbit. It becomes an entirely different dog. Because Whippets do not follow well, they can be a nightmare to the lure operator. They are constantly trying to catch the lure, and often these dogs will end up in three different places, with the lure operator desperately trying to keep them from ending the course prematurely. They are exciting to watch in action, and so small that one person can easily transport five or six to a trial in a wagon that would only hold three of a larger breed.

OFFICIAL STANDARD FOR THE WHIPPET

General Appearance—A medium size sighthound giving the appearance of elegance and fitness, denoting great speed, power and balance without coarseness. A true sporting hound that covers a maximum of distance with a minimum of lost motion. Should convey an impression of beautifully balanced muscular power and strength, combined with great elegance and grace of outline. Symmetry of outline, muscular development and powerful gait are the main considerations; the dog being built for speed and work, all forms of exaggeration should be avoided.

Size, Proportion, Substance—Ideal height for dogs, 19 to 22 inches; for bitches, 18 to 21 inches, measured at the highest point of the withers. One-half inch above or below the stated limits will disqualify. Length from forechest to buttocks equal to or slightly greater than height at the withers. Moderate bone throughout.

Head—Keen intelligent alert expression. *Eyes* large and dark. Both eyes must be of the same color. Yellow or light eyes should be strictly penalized. Blue or wall eyes shall disqualify. Fully pigmented eyelids are desirable. Rose *ears*, small, fine in texture; in repose, thrown back and folded along neck. Fold should be maintained when at attention. Erect ears should be severely penalized. *Skull* long and lean, fairly wide between the ears, scarcely perceptible stop. *Muzzle* should be long and powerful, denoting great strength of bite, without coarseness. Lack of underjaw should be strictly penalized. *Nose* entirely black. *Teeth* of upper jaw should fit closely over teeth of lower jaw creating a scissors bite. Teeth should be white and strong. Undershot shall disqualify. Overshot one-quarter inch or more shall disqualify.

Neck, Topline, Body—Neck long, clean and muscular, well arched with no suggestion of throatiness, widening gracefully into the top of the shoulder. A short thick neck, or a ewe neck, should be penalized. The *back* is broad, firm

These Whippets leave no doubt about wanting the run to begin.

"See you at the finish line!"

and well muscled, having length over the loin. The backline runs smoothly from the withers with a graceful natural arch, not too accentuated, beginning over the loin and carrying through over the croup; the arch is continuous without flatness. A dip behind shoulder blades, wheelback, flat back, or a steep or flat croup should be penalized. *Brisket* very deep, reaching as nearly as possible to the point of the elbow. *Ribs* well sprung but with no suggestion of barrel shape. The space between the forelegs is filled in so that there is no appearance of a hollow between them. There is a definite tucking of the underline. The *tail* long and tapering, reaching to the hipbone when drawn through between the hind legs. When the dog is in motion, the tail is carried low with only a gentle upward curve; tail should not be carried higher than top of back.

Forequarters—*Shoulder blade* long, well laid back, with flat muscles, allowing for moderate space between shoulder blades at peak of withers. Upper arm of equal length, placed so that the elbow falls directly under the withers. The points of the elbows should point neither in nor out, but straight back. A steep shoulder, short upper arm, a heavily muscled or loaded shoulder, or a very narrow shoulder, all of which restrict low free movement, should be strictly penalized. *Forelegs* straight, giving appearance of strength and substance of bone. Pasterns strong, slightly bent and flexible. Bowed legs, tied-in elbows, legs lacking substance, legs set far under the body so as to create an exaggerated forechest, weak or upright pasterns should be strictly penalized. Both front and rear feet must be well formed with hard, thick pads. Feet more hare than cat, but both are acceptable. Flat, splayed or soft feet without thick hard pads should be strictly penalized. Toes should be long, close and well arched. Nails strong and naturally short or of moderate length. Dewclaws may be removed.

Hindquarters—Long and powerful. The thighs are broad and muscular, stifles well bent; muscles are long and flat and carry well down toward the hock. The hocks are well let down and close to the ground. Sickle or cow hocks should be strictly penalized.

Coat—Short, close, smooth and firm in texture. Any other coat shall be a disqualification. Old scars and injuries, the result of work or accident, should not be allowed to prejudice the dog's chance in the show ring.

Color—Color immaterial.

Gait—Low, free moving and smooth, with reach in the forequarters and strong drive in the hindquarters. The dog has great freedom of action when viewed from the side; the forelegs move forward close to the ground to give a long low reach; the hind legs have strong propelling power. When moving and viewed from front or rear, legs should turn neither in nor out, nor should feet cross or interfere with each other. Lack of front reach or rear drive, or a short, hackney gait with high wrist action, should be strictly penalized. Crossing in front or moving too close should be strictly penalized.

Temperament—Amiable, friendly, gentle, but capable of great intensity during sporting pursuits.

DISQUALIFICATIONS

One-half inch above or below stated height limits.
Blue or wall eyes.
Undershot, overshot one-quarter inch or more.
Any coat other than short, close, smooth and firm in texture.

Approved December 11, 1989

Salukis straining to be off.

4

Lure-Coursing Programs, Rules and Regulations

THE AMERICAN SIGHTHOUND FIELD ASSOCIA-
TION (ASFA) was formed on May 21, 1972, with Lyle Gillette as
President. Since then, the officers and club delegates have met each
year in a different part of the country. At these meetings, changes in
the rules and regulations are made to benefit the sport. The ASFA setup
at present provides for an open stake for all hounds that have not yet
acquired their field championships and another stake for field champions of record. Then the winners of these two stakes meet to determine
Best of Breed. After this has been done, there is another draw, and the
Best of Breed winners are run in duos or trios to determine Best in
Field. One of the two rule changes made in 1989 was the introduction
of a singles stake open to untried hounds whose owners wish to compete. No points are awarded for this stake, but it is valuable for owners
of hounds who find it difficult to locate practice meets. The second
change was to approve the Lure Coursing Master (LCM) infinity rule.
This makes it possible for hounds that already have the LCM title to
run for LCM-II, LCM-III and on into infinity. This was done, of

course, to keep good hounds running and to give them added recognition.

The point schedule for ASFA events is given here even though it appears in the rules and regulations later in this chapter because it differs greatly from that of American Kennel Club lure coursing. First place gives points equaling four times the number of hounds competing in the stake with a maximum of forty points. Second place gives three times the number of hounds competing, with a maximum of thirty points, third place gives twice the number of hounds competing with a maximum of twenty points and fourth place points are equal to the number of hounds competing, with a maximum of ten points. There is also a Next Best Qualified (NBQ) with no points being awarded. No hound that does not score at least 50 percent of the total possible combined scores receives a placement or is awarded points.

According to the ASFA rules, a field championship is awarded when a hound has attained 100 points. In this 100 points, there must be two first placements or one first and two second placements with competition, which means defeating at least one placing hound. The Lure Courser of Merit title requires at least 300 points, including four firsts with competition.

The AKC has been interested in the sport of lure coursing for a number of years, but it wasn't until 1991 that the Performance Events Department was able to institute a program. When they did this, the AKC appropriated the present ASFA clubs and all of the ASFA-licensed judges and allowed them to hold AKC lure trials. The AKC also adopted the majority of ASFA's rules and regulations, but there are still important differences in the way the two organizations award points for field championships and the stakes being run. The AKC also awards the title of Junior Courser (JC) to hounds running successfully alone and the title of Senior Courser (SC) to those running in competition, even without placing in the stake.

To become a Junior Courser, a hound must complete a course of at least 600 yards with four turns. It must do this at two different trials and under more than one judge. It receives a green qualifying ribbon for each course. For the Senior Courser title, the hound must run with at least one other hound and must receive qualifying scores at two AKC trials under two different judges.

For its field championship, the AKC has laid out a schedule of points similar to the format for its dog shows. The hound must win fifteen championship points, and included in those points must be two first placements of three points or more (majors) under two different judges or pairs of judges. For a five-point major there must be an entry of twenty Whippets. Afghans, Basenjis, Borzois, and Salukis need ten, and the remainder of the hounds need eight. For a four- or three-point major, the number of hounds decreases somewhat, but for some breeds it is still difficult to gather the number of hounds needed. The AKC runs only one stake for each breed—the open. The winner of that stake is entitled to run for Best in Field, and this is the great equalizer. The winner of BIF receives the highest total of points for any breed also running for BIF. In other words, if there are twenty Whippets entered and the Best of Breed (BB) Whippet runs for BIF, and this honor goes to an Ibizan Hound with only one entered in the trial, the Ibizan also receives five points. That evens the point situation somewhat, but it remains much more difficult to obtain an AKC field championship than it is for a hound to become an ASFA field champion.

On the other hand, an AKC trial can be run much faster than one for the ASFA because the former has only one stake (open) while the ASFA has at least three (open, FC and a runoff between the two winners). When AKC tests are held in conjunction with trials, the JC test is on a pass-or-fail basis with no scoring, so it does not take the judge long to score. The time element of the trials is important, especially during the season of standard time, as the daylight evaporates rather quickly. Even to receive one point in an AKC trial there must be an entry of at least three hounds in all breeds except Whippets, where six are needed. This makes it quite difficult for the less popular breeds to find enough competition to garner even one point after traveling a long distance to attend a trial. On the other hand, ASFA offers four points even if the hound runs alone successfully, and it can also attain a first with competition if it goes BIF.

Those are the main differences in the rules and regulations of the ASFA and the AKC. Following you will find the complete rules and regulations for both groups, and you may judge for yourself. Personally, I think changes for the better in the point situation would be beneficial to both. The AKC is obviously much too difficult due to the scarcity of hounds in competition, and the ASFA is too easy as long as you attend enough trials. It is my hope that in time both these situations will be resolved and that they will have one point system agreeable to both groups.

AMERICAN KENNEL CLUB REGULATIONS FOR LURE COURSING TESTS AND TRIALS

Chapter I

SECTION 1. PURPOSE. The purpose of noncompetitive lure coursing tests is to offer sighthound breed owners a standardized gauge to measure their hounds' coursing instinct.

The purpose of the competitive lure coursing trial program is to preserve and develop the coursing skills inherent in the sighthounds and to demonstrate that they can perform the functions for which they were originally bred.

Although lure coursing events are artificial simulations of coursing, they are designed to measure and develop the characteristics of the sighthound breeds.

LURE COURSING TESTS AND TRIALS ARE SPORTS AND ALL PARTICIPANTS MUST BE GUIDED BY THE PRINCIPLES OF GOOD SPORTSMANSHIP BOTH ON AND OFF THE TEST AND TRIAL FIELDS.

SECTION 2. LURE COURSING TESTS AND TRIALS DEFINED. A MEMBER LURE COURSING TEST is a test at which certifications toward titles are awarded, given by a club or association which is a member of The American Kennel Club.

A MEMBER LURE COURSING TRIAL is a trial at which qualifying scores and championship points toward titles are awarded, given by a club or association which is a member of The American Kennel Club.

A LICENSED LURE COURSING TEST is a test at which certifications toward titles are awarded, given by a club or association which is not a member of The American Kennel Club, but which has been licensed by The American Kennel Club to give the coursing test.

A LICENSED LURE COURSING TRIAL is a trial at which qualifying scores and championship points toward titles are awarded, given by a club or association which is not a member of The American Kennel Club, but which has been licensed by The American Kennel Club to give the specific lure coursing trial designated in the license.

Sanctioned LURE COURSING TESTS and TRIALS are informal events at which hounds may participate, but not for titles, held by a club or association by obtaining the sanction of The American Kennel Club.

SECTION 3. ELIGIBILITY OF SIGHTHOUNDS. Only pure-bred Afghan Hounds, Basenjis, Borzois, Greyhounds, Ibizan Hounds, Irish Wolfhounds, Pharaoh Hounds, Rhodesian Ridgebacks, Salukis, Scottish Deerhounds and Whippets, that are one year of age or older and that have been registered with the American Kennel Club or that have been granted an Indefinite Listing Privilege (ILP), are eligible to participate in lure coursing tests and trials.

Spayed and neutered, hounds are eligible to participate. Monorchid and cryptorchid hounds are ineligible to participate.

SECTION 4. BREED DISQUALIFICATIONS. Hounds with breed disqualifications, as listed in the AKC Breed Standards, are ineligible to enter lure coursing trials and tests.

PHARAOH HOUNDS—Any solid white spot on the back of neck, shoulder, or any part of the back or sides of the dog.

SCOTTISH DEERHOUNDS—White blaze on head or a white collar.

WHIPPETS—Blue or wall eyes;

Undershot; overshot one-quarter inch or more.

Size: dogs 19 to 22 inches; bitches 18 to 21 inches; both to be measured across the shoulders at the highest point; one-half inch above or below the stated measurements will disqualify.

Coat: any coat other than short, close, smooth and firm in texture.

SECTION 5. RULES APPLYING TO REGISTRATION AND DISCIPLINE. Chapters 3 and 3A of The American Kennel Club's Rules Applying to Registration and Dog Shows shall apply to all events held under these Regulations.

Chapters 22 and 23 of The American Kennel Club's Rules Applying to Registration and Dog Shows shall apply to all coursing tests and trials held under AKC Regulations.

The power conferred by Chapter 22 Section 2 to suspend a person from all privileges of The American Kennel Club applies only to committees at licensed or member events. At a sanctioned event, the committee collects evidence, holds a hearing, if warranted, and reports its finding and conclusions to The American Kennel Club.

SECTION 6. RISK. The owner or a handler entering a hound in a test or trial does so at his or her own risk and agrees to assume responsibility for any damage to facilities or persons, caused by him or her or by his or her hound(s). He or she also agrees to abide by the Rules of The American Kennel Club and these Regulations.

Chapter II

SECTION 1. ELIGIBILITY TO HOLD LURE COURSING TESTS AND TRIALS. The Board of Directors of The American Kennel Club may, at its discretion, grant permission to a club or association to hold six (6) lure coursing tests and/or four (4) lure coursing trials per year which shall be governed by such Regulations as from time to time shall be approved by the Board of Directors.

SECTION 2. MAKING APPLICATION. A club or association, that meets the requirements of The American Kennel Club, that wishes to hold a lure coursing test and/or trial at which qualifying scores toward titles or championship points may be earned, must make application to The American Kennel Club on the form provided for permission to hold the event. An application fee of $20.00 per event must accompany each application.

If the club or association fails to hold its event at the approved time and place, the amount of the application fee paid will be returned. If circumstances prior to the first day of an event require a club to cancel the event, or to change the approved location, the event-giving club must notify the AKC, in advance, if possible.

Applications for licensed and member club lure coursing tests and lure coursing trials must be received by the AKC at least ninety (90) days prior to the date(s) of the event. A club may be approved to hold a lure coursing test and lure coursing trial on the same day(s).

A club or association that meets all of the requirements of The American Kennel Club may be approved to hold a sanctioned test or trial by applying on a form provided by The American Kennel Club and paying an application fee. Sanctioned test and trial applications must be received by the AKC at least four weeks prior to the date(s) of the event(s).

A club or association that has held a trial or trials in any one year shall have first right to claim the corresponding date(s) for its trial(s) to be held in the next succeeding year. However, Priority Dates will only be held 120 days without a request from the Host Club with priority.

All-breed trials on the same date must be no less than 150 miles apart.

A club must hold a minimum of one trial every other year to remain active with the AKC.

The license to hold a Lure Field Trial is granted for a specified time period. The host club shall not, under any circumstances, complete a trial at a future date.

All of these Regulations shall govern sanctioned events except those which specifically state that they apply to a member or licensed event.

SECTION 3. ENTRY FEES, REFUNDS. Entry fees shall be fixed by the Host Club and shall be forfeited in such cases where hounds are scratched from the field for causes, except as follows:

(a) Hounds determined to be lame or to have a breed disqualification at the time of Roll Call shall be barred from competition and their entry fees shall be refunded.

(b) Bitches in season, or which come in season after the close of entries, shall be barred from participating and their entry fee shall be refunded. Notification to the Field Secretary of bitches in season must be made before or during the Roll Call. Bitches known to be in season shall not be brought onto the trial grounds.

SECTION 4. DETRIMENTAL SUBSTANCES. There shall be no consumption of any type of alcoholic beverages or illegal drugs by any Judge, any member of the Field committee or by anyone working in any official capacity prior to the completion of their assignment. Said consumption shall be deemed detrimental to the sport of Lure Field Trials.

SECTION 5. RULE INTERPRETATION. The Board of Directors of The American Kennel Club shall have authority to issue, from time to time, where necessary, notices that amplify, clarify, or interpret these running rules.

Chapter III

SECTION 1. APPOINTMENT OF LURE COURSING TEST AND TRIAL COMMITTEE. A club or association that has been granted permission by The American Kennel Club to hold a test or trial must appoint a lure coursing test or trial committee which will have complete responsibility for the planning and conduct of the event.

The premium list shall list the names of all officials. In addition the addresses of the Chairman and Secretary shall be included. The Field Committee shall consist of no less than five individuals who shall fill the positions of:

Field Chairman,
Field Secretary,
Field Clerk,
Huntmaster,
Lure Operator,
Inspection and Measuring Committee.

This committee will insure the efficient and orderly conduct of the event. The committee is responsible for compliance with all of these regulations except for those coming under the sole jurisdiction of the judge(s).

The Committee has the authority to decide upon any matter arising during the running of the event, except those matters coming within the jurisdiction of the judge(s).

The Committee shall be responsible for the duties enumerated in the following sections which may be delegated as appropriate.

SECTION 2. FIELD SECRETARY.
(Must be a member of the host club)

1. Is a member of the Field Committee.

2. Applies for a date to hold a trial and/or test.

3. Schedules Judging assignments. Solicits in writing, and receives in writing, confirmation of those Judging assignments prior to submitting the Premium List for approval. A copy of the confirmation shall be made available to The American Kennel Club upon request.

4. Prepares and mails out premium lists and entry forms, after receiving official approval, and accepts entries.

5. Any Field Secretary or host club which accepts an entry fee other than that published in its premium list, or in any way discriminates between entrants, shall be disciplined. All persons found guilty of paying or receiving any monies, special inducements or allowances in violation of the foregoing shall be disciplined.

6. The Field Secretary may decline any entries for cause, but in each and every such instance the Club shall file good and sufficient reasons for so doing with the AKC.

7. The Field Secretary shall decline any late, incomplete, unsigned, unpaid or conditional entries. Each entry must be completed in full and the information given on the form must be that which applies

to that entered hound. The entry form must be signed by the owner or agent duly authorized to make the entry.

8. Provides the Field Chairman with a list of hounds entered for the purpose of Roll Call.

9. Shall have available a copy of the current edition of this book for the use of the Field Committee and all other officials.

10. Insures that all record sheets and forms are available and forwarded with recording fees to reach the AKC, or be postmarked within nine (9) days of the meet.

11. Is responsible for the draw of hounds in competition.

SECTION 3. FIELD CHAIRMAN.

(Must be a member of the host club)

1. Is chairman of the Field Committee.

2. Provides the grounds for the meet.

3. Shall appoint an inspection and measuring committee who shall have the responsibility of inspecting all hounds entered. (See Section 7, this Chapter.)

4. Carries out a Roll Call of entered hounds.

5. Insures that all equipment is in place and functioning, including proper color and size blankets.

6. Insures that all placement awards are on hand.

7. Provides for policing, i.e., clean-up of the grounds before, during and after the meet, especially of anything remotely resembling a lure and anything hazardous.

8. Must individually approve anyone who is to be allowed in the judging area other than the Officials of the trial (e.g., apprentice judges).

9. May at his discretion excuse from the field for the day any hound that exhibits uncontrolled aggressive behavior toward any person or hound on the trial grounds, except hounds competing in the course then in progress. The Field Chairman may levy and collect a penalty fee of $5.00 from the owner or his duly authorized agent of any hound that is loose on the field and not in competition at the time.

10. Will lay out the course according to the approved course plan.

11. Shall announce the final placements and scores at the end of the stake or trial.

SECTION 4. FIELD CLERK.

1. Is a member of the Field Committee.

2. Shall be stationed on the field and shall promptly collect the

score sheets from the Judges upon the completion of the judging of each course.

3. Posts the scores on the Record Sheets. The Field Clerk(s) shall notify the Judge of a mathematical error and said error shall be corrected and initialed by the Judge. The Field Clerk(s) shall not change any Judge's scores (see Chapter IV, Sec. 13).

4. Posts preliminary scores of each breed before finals, final scores before run-offs and Best of Breed runs and Best of Breed scores before Best in Field runs.

SECTION 5. HUNTMASTER.

1. Is a member of the Field Committee.

2. Will be in complete charge of all hounds and handlers.

3. Shall call up each new course as each previous course is completed.

4. Will insure that a handler handles only one hound in each course.

5. Must explain release and retrieval procedures before each preliminary course only.

6. Shall stand in close proximity to, but not in front of, the handlers and hounds.

7. The lure must be positioned in front of the hounds and in the direction in which it will travel before the signal is given to activate it.

8. As the hounds are facing the lure, the hounds shall be placed as follows:

>YELLOW on the left.
>PINK in the middle or to the right in braces,
>BLUE on the right in trios.

9. Shall question in the following order the Judge, Lure Operator and handlers ''Are you ready,'' and after affirmative answers, the course is begun.

10. Provides a hand signal to the Lure Operator to start the lure.

11. Gives the signal ''Tally-Ho'' to release the hounds for each course, and ''Retrieve your Hounds'' when appropriate.

12. Hounds should not be slipped before the sound of the ''T'' in ''Tally-Ho.'' Will notify the Judge and handler of any pre-slip at the end of the course. If the Huntmaster fails to notify the Judge of a pre-slip, then to all intents there has been no pre-slip, but the Judge shall have the prerogative to question the Huntmaster if the release seems questionable.

13. Will cause the lure to be stopped upon a pre-slip and restart provided no Tally-Ho has been sounded. (The pre-slip penalty will carry over.)

14. Will inspect the lure before every course and replace it if needed.

15. Will neither pick up nor authorize anyone to pick up or touch the lure until such time as all hounds have completed the course and are under the control of their handlers.

16. Shall notify the Trial Chairman of any hound which appears lame.

17. Shall immediately inform the handlers in a course that is called a no-course or a course in which a dog is dismissed or disqualified.

SECTION 6. LURE OPERATOR.

1. Is a member of the Field Committee.

2. Will make at least one pilot run of the lure before the first course of the day and there again upon reversing or changing the course layout.

3. Starts the lure at the signal from the Huntmaster and stops it at least 20 yards before the lure machine or the final pulley.

4. Will attempt to keep the lure 10 to 30 yards in front of the lead hound at all times after the course begins. In the event a hound becomes unsighted, the lure must continue in the originally planned direction until completion of the course.

5. Will stop the lure on a signal from the Huntmaster or Judge, but shall automatically stop the lure any time a hound becomes entangled in the string or when a potentially dangerous situation may develop.

6. Shall not operate the lure for any stake where any hound which he owns or co-owns or is owned or co-owned by a member of his immediate family or household is entered.

7. The same Lure Operator shall operate the lure throughout an entire stake.

SECTION 7. INSPECTION AND MEASURING COMMITTEE.

1. Are members of the Field Committee.

2. The Inspection and Measuring Committee shall inspect each entry for lameness, bitches in season and breed disqualifications, at Roll Call.

3. Any entry found to be lame, have a breed disqualification,

or bitches in season shall be barred from competition and entry fees shall be refunded.

4. The procedure for measuring is as follows:

(a) The hound being measured shall be placed on a flat level surface that is not slippery. The handler shall position the hound at the Inspection Committee's discretion. The hound shall be in a naturally alert position, with the head up but not stretched upward, and with its feet well under it and its forelegs vertical as viewed both from the front and side.

(b) A member of the Inspection Committee shall first determine the highest point over the shoulder blades with one hand, and shall then pass the measuring wicket over the hound from the rear with the other hand, and place the wicket so the cross piece comes down directly on the highest point over the shoulder blades. The wicket should not be placed on the neck in front of the shoulder or on the spinal column behind the shoulder blades. At least two members of the Inspection Committee must agree that a hound is within or outside the height limits.

(c) All Whippets will be measured only once and at the time of roll call at each and every Field Trial, with the exception that Whippets that have been awarded the Field Champion title shall not be measured.

(d) Handlers will be allowed only two minutes to position their hounds in a proper standing position. Hounds that cannot be made to stand in the proper position for measurement within the allotted time will not be allowed to course, and their entry fees will be refunded.

SECTION 8. FIELD COMMITTEE.

1. Field Committees may make additional regulations for the government of their events as shall be considered necessary and proper, provided such regulations or rules do not conflict with, change or modify any running regulations of The American Kennel Club. Such additional regulations shall be printed and distributed with the premium list and violations thereof shall be considered the same as violations of the Rules and Regulations of the AKC.

2. The decision of the Field Committee shall be final, conclusive and binding on all parties, in all matters occurring on the day of the meet, except for matters coming within the jurisdiction of the Judge(s). Such Committee decisions must be made in accord with the general regulations and standard procedures that apply to the trial being held.

3. The decision of the Judges in all matters relating to the course is final and binding.

4. If it becomes necessary to replace an advertised Judge after

the opening of the event and no person on the eligible judges list is available as a replacement, the Field Committee may select a person whose name is not on the eligible judges list provided such person is in good standing with the AKC. The Field Committee must announce the name of any substitute Judge before the draw for the stake at which he is to officiate.

5. If a Judge is unable to complete a Judging assignment a replacement may be substituted. The Field Committee shall notify the exhibitors of the substitution. All of the scores of the Judge who was replaced shall stand as recorded.

6. If a Judge is substituted the owner or handler of a hound entered in that stake has the option of withdrawing the hound before the draw and receiving his entry fee back. If, after the draw, a Judge must be substituted, no refunds shall be made.

7. In the event that an unadvertised Lure Operator must be used the Field Committee must select a substitute Lure Operator and must announce the name of that substitute before the draw for the stake at which he is to operate the lure. If an unadvertised Lure Operator is used, the owner or handler of a hound entered in that stake has the option of withdrawing his hound before the draw and receiving his entry fee back. If, subsequent to the draw, a Lure Operator must be substituted, no refunds shall be made. The advertised Lure Operator shall make every effort to complete his assignment.

8. The Field Committee shall handle all official protests on the day of the event as specified in Chapter XIII.

9. At no time may the Field Committee overrule, change or reverse a judging decision except in case of eligibility as determined after a protest is filed without the express consent in writing of the Judge involved.

Chapter IV
Judging

In addition to those Regulations and procedures set forth in Chapter II, as they relate to Judges, the following shall apply:

SECTION 1. JUDGING. Each Breed will be judged by one or two Judges, at the option of the Host Club.

SECTION 2. JUDGES HANDLING HOUNDS. No Judge shall handle a hound in the stake or stakes where he is officiating, nor shall a hound belonging to any Judge or his immediate family or household be entered in any stake where that Judge is officiating. Such hounds may be entered at that meet in other stakes where the Judge is not officiating. A Judge cannot stop judging a stake to handle a hound in another stake.

SECTION 3. WALKING THE COURSE. Each and every Judge, before beginning his assignment, shall walk the course and verify with the Field Chairman that an approved course plan is properly staked, and free of hazards in so far as possible.

SECTION 4. DISCUSSION DURING JUDGING. While on the field during his judging assignment, no Judge shall discuss anything relative to his judging assignment with any handler or agent.

SECTION 5. CALLING A NO-COURSE. A Judge shall be able to call a no-course for the following reasons:
(a) the hounds are interfered with, disrupted, or he cannot fairly score the course.
(b) when a segment of the lure falls off and any hound reacts to said segment, but only if he cannot fairly score the course.
(c) if a hound or hounds touch or catch the lure and, in the Judge's opinion, by so doing that action causes interference with the running of the course, it shall be declared a no-course. Anytime a hound becomes entangled in the string, the Judge shall order the lure stopped and may declare a no-course.
(d) if the Lure Operator fails to maintain the 10–30 yards limit, and the hounds become unsighted, the Judge shall have the prerogative to call a no-course.

SECTION 6. SCORING. Judges are responsible for scoring all categories in all courses in the preliminaries, finals, run-offs, etc.

Scoring and placing of winners shall be decided on the basis of qualities evidenced by: Overall Ability, Follow, Speed, Agility and Endurance. Judges shall score in whole numbers only, and shall be governed by the following system:

Overall Ability .... 10 points

Follow 10

Speed 10

Agility 10

86

Endurance 10

Total .... 50 points

Less: Pre-slip penalty 1 to 5 points

When a pre-slip occurs, the Judge shall levy a penalty of 1 to 5 points for that course. The pre-slip penalty shall be carried over in the case where a no-course is called on the course in progress.

Less: Course delay penalty 1 to 5 points

When a course delay occurs, the Judge shall levy a 1 to 5 point penalty against the hound causing the delay. The course delay penalty shall be carried over in the case where a no-course is called on the course in progress and shall be cumulative in the case of repeated delays.

SECTION 7. ZERO SCORE. A zero total score in the preliminary course automatically excuses a hound for the day. The hound shall be considered as not having been in competition when computing points.

SECTION 8. EXCUSALS. Hounds may be excused from the field, by either Judge, for the following reasons:

(a) Hounds who fail to run after the Tally-Ho in the preliminary course.

(b) Hounds which course other hounds rather than the lure.

(c) Hounds who delay the course.

SECTION 9. DISMISSAL. Hounds shall be dismissed from the field, by either Judge, for the day, for interfering (aggressively or playfully) with the course of another hound. (Growling and/or barking, in and of itself, does not constitute grounds for dismissal.)

SECTION 10. DISQUALIFICATION. Hounds shall be disqualified, by either Judge, for an aggressive attack towards another hound on the field. (Barking and/or growling, in itself does not constitute aggression.) A hound should not be disqualified for defending itself when attacked.

SECTION 11. RERUN. If a hound is excused, dismissed or disqualified, the course may be called a no-course. The remaining hound or hounds may be run in a remaining course if one exists or be given the opportunity to re-run alone and be scored.

Judges may score some hounds in a course and rerun other hounds from the same course. At their discretion, Judges may score hounds which fail to complete the course for any reason, if a Judge is able to do so.

SECTION 12. NOTIFYING THE HUNTMASTER. Judges shall immediately inform the Huntmaster when a course is called a no-course or when a hound is dismissed or disqualified. (Chapter III, Section 5, #17.)

SECTION 13. REASON FOR DISQUALIFICATION, DISMISSAL AND EXCUSAL. Judges must state on the Judges Sheet the specific reason for excusal, dismissal or disqualification.

SECTION 14. CHANGING SCORES. After a course has been judged, and the marked score sheets turned over to the Field Clerk, only the Judge can change his final score and only in the case of a mathematical or blanket color error.

SECTION 15. JUDGES' DECISIONS ARE FINAL. The Judge's decisions upon all matters relating to the course and the merits of the hounds are final and binding.

Chapter V
Veterinarian

The club shall have one or more veterinarians on call and must insure that veterinary assistance will be available within a reasonable time should it be needed.

Chapter VI
Removal from Lure Coursing Test or Trial

A Trial or Test Committee may remove any hound from the grounds for cause. In each such instance the club shall file good and sufficient reasons for so doing with The American Kennel Club.

A Trial or Test Committee may ask a person to leave the grounds and shall also employ disciplinary action per AKC procedures. (See Chapter 22, Section 2, AKC Rules Applying to Registration and Dog Shows.)

Chapter VII
Ribbons and Rosettes

SECTION 1. TESTS. A club or association holding a licensed or member club lure coursing test shall offer a ribbon or rosette to each dog that receives a certification.

Each ribbon or rosette shall be at least two inches wide and approximately eight inches long and shall bear on its face a facsimile of the seal of The American Kennel Club, the words "Lure Coursing Test," "Qualifying Course," and the name of the test-giving club or association. Ribbons and rosettes shall be dark green in color, and rosettes shall have a white center streamer and white button.

If ribbons or rosettes are awarded at sanctioned lure coursing tests, they shall be awarded only to hounds receiving certification and shall be light green.

SECTION 2. TRIALS. A club or association holding a licensed or member club lure coursing trial shall offer prize ribbons or rosettes for all placements. Each ribbon or rosette shall be at least two inches wide and approximately eight inches long, and shall bear on its face a facsimile of the seal of The American Kennel Club, the words "Lure Coursing Trial," the name of the prize (first, second, etc.), and the name of the trial-giving club or association.

The colors of the ribbons or rosettes for the stakes and Best in Field shall be:

* First Place	Blue
* Second Place	Red
* Third Place	Yellow
* Fourth Place	White
* Fifth Place	Pink
* Best of Breed	Purple and Gold
* Best In Field	Red, White and Blue

Trophies may be awarded to any or all placements and to hounds receiving qualifying scores at lure coursing trials.

If ribbons or rosettes are awarded at sanctioned lure coursing trials, they shall be awarded only to placing hounds receiving qualifying scores and shall be the following colors:

* First	Rose
* Second	Brown
* Third	Light Green
* Fourth	Gray
* Fifth	Orange

* Best of Breed

* Best In Field

Lavender and White

Pink and Green

Chapter VIII
Premium Lists

SECTION 1. SAMPLE COPIES. Two sample copies of the Premium List and entry form must be sent to the AKC postmarked at least 60 days prior to the approved date. A Field Secretary may not mail out the Premium List until such time as it has been approved for mailing by the AKC.

SECTION 2. ELIGIBLE JUDGES. Only those persons whose names appear on the list of eligible judges of the AKC may be approved to judge at licensed or member lure field trials.

SECTION 3. COURSE PLANS. Exact layouts, including approximate distances between turns, and locations of hills, gullies, fences, etc., of proposed coursing plans must be in the Premium List.

1. No course shall be less than 600 yards.

2. When using a continuous loop system the lure must not traverse the course twice in order to meet the distance requirements. The minimum distance of line used on the continuous loop shall be 600 yards.

3. When using a continuous loop system, midcourse reversals are not permissible.

SECTION 4. ENTRY FORMS. Must conform to the sample printed in this book. Must include front and back. Entry form must be signed by owner or owner's agent.

SECTION 5. PREMIUM LIST.

(A) GENERAL.

A Premium List must be provided for licensed or member club lure coursing tests and or trials. The Premium List shall be printed (any printing or copying process is acceptable), and shall state whether the event is "Licensed by The American Kennel Club" or held by an "AKC Member Club." Premium Lists shall measure not less than 5½ × 8½ inches nor more than 8½ × 11 inches.

Each trial shall have a separate Premium List.

Only information pertaining to that trial shall be included on the Premium List. Separate enclosures mailed with the Premium List are acceptable.

Four copies of the printed Premium List for licensed or member club tests and trials must be mailed to the AKC at the time they are mailed or distributed to prospective entrants.

(B) TESTS/TRIALS.

The following information shall be included in the Premium List for a licensed or member lure coursing test and or trial:

(1) name of club or association offering the event.
(2) the exact location and date of the event,
(3) name and address of the Test and or Trial Committee Chairman,
(4) Name, address and telephone number of the Test and or Trial Secretary,
(5) the names of the Test and or Trial Committee members (minimum of five including Chairman),
(6) time event(s) will commence,
(7) entry fees,
(8) event(s) offered,
(9) names and addresses of Judges together with their assignments,
(10) date and time of closing and drawing of entries,
(11) a listing of club officers,
(12) the official AKC entry form,
(13) the statement ''Permission has been granted by the American Kennel Club for the holding of this event under American Kennel Club Rules and Regulations,''
(14) additional information, directions, dinner, etc.

Premium Lists shall also include the name, address and telephone number of the veterinarian(s) on call or on duty during the test/trial, and specify whether ribbons or rosettes will be awarded. Premium Lists should also describe any trophies that may be awarded and name the placements to which they will be awarded. Alcoholic beverages are not acceptable as prizes.

SECTION 6. CLOSING OF ENTRIES. Entries for a licensed or member club test or trial must close at the time specified in the Premium List.

If entries are to be limited, the numerical limitation(s) must be stated in the Premium List and entries will close when the numerical limit(s) have been reached.

A club or association holding a licensed or member lure coursing test or trial shall not accept any entries received after the closing time and date specified in the Premium List.

Each entry form must be completed in full and signed, and the information given on the entry form must be that which applies to the entered hound. Separate entry forms must be completed for each hound entered in a test or trial.

Chapter IX
Running the Meet Trial and Test Programs

SECTION 1. OPEN STAKE. Open to all hounds of a breed that have obtained at least one of the following:

    a. AKC Junior Courser title.
    b. American Sighthound Field Association Field Champion title.
    c. Canadian Kennel Club Field Champion title.
    d. American Kennel Club Field Champions of record of that breed may be entered.
    e. Hounds that are disqualified from AKC, ASFA or CKC Field Trials may not be entered.

SECTION 2. SPECIAL STAKE. Open to all hounds that are eligible to enter the open stake and have earned their AKC Field Championships titles. No championship points will be awarded from this stake.

SECTION 3. STAKES. The following applies to all stakes:

(1) Every entry in a stake, not excused, dismissed, or disqualified, shall be run twice. The order of running for both courses shall be by random draw. (See Sec. 4. below.)

(2) Hounds absent at Roll Call or at the running of their course shall be scratched, after a five- (5) minute grace period.

(3) After completion and posting of final scores, all hounds no longer required for further judging are excused.

(4) The top five placing hounds in each stake shall be determined by the combined scores of the preliminary and final runs.

(5) Ties for the top five placements in any stake will be run off or forfeited. If one hound in a tie runoff is dismissed or disqualified, the hound not dismissed or disqualified is considered to have won the runoff.

(6) The highest placing hound in each stake will compete in a Best of Breed runoff to determine that breed's Best of Breed. If there was only one breed stake, the winner of that stake will be awarded Best of Breed.

(7) All hounds entered in a given stake shall be divided into trios, if possible, or braces. Hounds shall be designated by colors according to their drawing.

First number drawn .... bright YELLOW
(place on left)

Second number drawn .... bright PINK
(middle or on the right in braces)

Third number drawn .... bright BLUE
(place on right)

SECTION 4. CONDUCTING THE DRAW. The running order of the hounds in all stakes shall be established by a random drawing. The draw will be conducted at the time and on the date specified in the Premium List for the closing and drawing of entries, and is open to all who wish to attend.

The Coursing Secretary or Chairman shall officiate over the draw.

1. Each hound shall be assigned a number and the order and arrangement of hounds coursing shall be determined by a random drawing of those numbers by breed at the time of the draw.

2. Upon request from an owner or owner's agent at roll call, multiple entries from an owner shall be divided as evenly as possible between the courses. This does not apply to the Best in Field Competition.

3. When there is but a single course in a regular stake in which an owner or his duly authorized agent has more than one hound, these hounds will be run together or one or more will be scratched by the owner or his duly authorized agent, without refund of entry fee.

4. If only one member of a breed is entered, that hound may be run with another breed if all the handlers involved agree. The hounds would be scored and placed separately.

5. A hound that has received a minimum score of less than half the total possible points in the preliminary course shall be eligible to compete in the final course. A hound that is excused will not be permitted to run in the final course, and will not be counted as having been in competition when computing the points.

6. After the draw is completed, should for any reason a hound fail to appear within the five- (5) minute grace period for its course, such that a single hound remains to be run, that remaining hound will be run and scored alone, unless that hound can be added to a brace, should one exist, in a remaining course.

SECTION 5. BEST IN FIELD. At the option of the host club a Best in Field may be offered. All Best of Breed winners shall be eligible to compete in the Best in Field competition. If the host club offers this competition, it must so indicate in the Premium List.

(1) Each hound will be run once, in a trio if possible, or brace. In the case of a tie for Best in Field the hounds will run-off or forfeit.

(2) The order of running is to be determined by random draw.

(3) Multiple entries from one owner will not be split into separate courses, if drawn together.

(4) The highest scoring hound will be declared the Best in Field winner on that day, and will be awarded points equal to the maximum number of points awarded to any hound defeated in this competition.

(5) An excusal, dismissal, or disqualification in the Best in Field competition will not affect a hound's prior awards earned on that day, but will count towards barring the hound from competition.

(6) A single entry in a breed receiving a qualifying score in a Best in Field competition will receive a certification towards the Senior Courser title.

SECTION 6. HANDLERS.

1. A person may handle any number of hounds during a trial, but may not handle more than one hound in each course of that trial.

2. Any owner who deputizes another person to handle his hound must not interfere with the hound or handler throughout the duration of the course.

3. Handlers shall provide each hound with a simplified slip lead which will give almost instantaneous freedom to the hound when the "Tally-Ho" signal is called by the Huntmaster.

4. Recommended slip leads are those consisting of a leather or webbing strap with a wide collar and double or single rings.

5. No collar or paraphernalia shall be on the hound during the running of the course except the blanket. Protective coverings in colors other than those listed in this Chapter, Section 3, #7, are acceptable. Muzzles may be worn at owners' discretion. (Muzzles must not have

sharp, hard edges and must allow the hound to breathe.) Spike or prong collars, electronic or dummy devices are prohibited on the grounds of a test or trial.

Chapter X
Recording Fees

At every licensed and member club lure coursing test and trial held under these Regulations, a recording fee of $3.00 shall be required for every entry. The recording fee is payable to The American Kennel Club and is to help defray expenses involved in maintaining the records, and applies to all entries, regardless of whether or not they participate, unless the entry fee is refunded per Chapter II, Section 3.

Chapter XI
Submission of Records

1. Clubs holding licensed or member tests or trials must utilize the standard American Kennel Club Official Report Forms which will be automatically supplied to the Lure Coursing Secretary following approval of the Premium List copy.

2. Postmarked within nine (9) days of the completion of a licensed or member club lure coursing test, the Test Secretary shall forward to the American Kennel Club the Official Reports containing the names and other identifying information for all hounds receiving a certification. The testers' sheets must be signed and certified by the Judge and the Test Secretary, and forwarded to the AKC with all entry forms, test score sheets, recording fees, and a catalog if one was prepared.

3. Postmarked within nine (9) days of the completion of a licensed or member club lure coursing trial, the Trial Secretary shall forward to The American Kennel Club the Official Reports containing the names and other identifying information for all placements and all hounds entered. The Judges' sheets must be signed and certified by the judge(s) and forwarded to the AKC with all entry forms, record sheets, recording fees and a catalog if one was prepared.

4. The American Kennel Club will correct errors and placements on record sheets, where appropriate, but will not change any Judge's total score. The American Kennel Club will notify the Field Secretary of the host club of any and all such changes.

5. A club or association holding a licensed or member lure cours-

ing test or trial shall retain a copy of the official record sheets for at least one year.

Chapter XII
Cancellation of Awards

If an ineligible hound has been entered and run in a licensed or member test or trial, or if the person or persons named as owner or owners on the entry form are not the person or persons who actually owned the hound at the time entries closed, or if a hound is run in a class for which it has not been entered, or if its entry form is deemed invalid by The American Kennel Club under the Rules or Regulations, all resulting qualifying scores and/or placements, as applicable, shall be cancelled by The American Kennel Club.

If a placement and/or qualifying score of a hound is cancelled by The American Kennel Club, the entrant of the hound shall return all prizes to the secretary of the trial- or test-giving club within ten (10) days of receipt of notice from The American Kennel Club of said cancellation.

If at a trial, a placement is cancelled, the hound next in order of merit shall be moved up, and the new placement of the hound moved up shall be counted the same as if it had received the original award.

Chapter XIII
Titles

SECTION 1. TESTING TITLES.
(Suffix to a hound's name)
1. JUNIOR COURSER (JC)
A hound running alone shall receive certification from a Judge on one date, and a second certification from a different Judge at a later date, stating that the hound completed a 600 yard course with a minimum of four (4) turns. The hound must complete the course with enthusiasm and without interruption. The two runs can be on the same date at or in conjunction with a National Breed Specialty.
2. SENIOR COURSER (SC)
(a) Must be eligible to enter the open stake. See Chapter IX, Section 1.
(b) The hound must run with at least one other hound.

(c) Must receive qualifying scores at two (2) AKC licensed or member trials, under two different Judges.

SECTION 2. FIELD CHAMPIONSHIP (F. CH.).
(Prefix to the hound's name)

Must obtain fifteen (15) championship points; included in these 15 points must be two first placements with three points or more, under two different Judges or judging panels.

Schedule of points by breed:

	First Place				
Points	**5**	**4**	**3**	**2**	**1**
Afghan Hounds	10	8	6	4	2
Basenjis	10	8	6	4	2
Borzois	10	8	6	4	2
Greyhounds	8	6	5	4	2
Ibizan Hounds	8	6	5	4	2
Irish Wolfhounds	8	6	5	4	2
Pharaoh Hounds	8	6	5	4	2
Salukis	10	8	6	4	2
Scottish Deerhounds	8	6	5	4	2
Rhodesian Ridgebacks	10	8	6	4	2
Whippets	18	12	9	6	2
When 1st place hound earns	5		4		3
The 2nd place hound earns	3		2		1
The 3rd place hound earns	2		1		0

Chapter XIV
Protests

SECTION 1. PROTEST AGAINST HOUNDS.

1. Any person who is a member of a member club of The American Kennel Club, or who owns a hound entered in the test or trial, or who handles a hound in the test or trial may make a protest to the test or trial committee against any participating hound either before or after the hound has run, alleging that it is ineligible to participate in the test

or trial in which it is entered. Such a protest shall be in writing, shall identify the hound protested and specify the basis for the protest, shall bear the signature and address of the person who makes it and shall describe his qualifications for making the protest. It shall be filed with the trial or test secretary or with the chairman of the committee before the completion of the event, and shall be accompanied by a deposit of $25.00, which shall be returned if the protest is sustained, or which will be forfeited if the protest is not sustained.

2. If such a protest is received, the committee shall hold a meeting as soon as possible. The person who made the protest must be present, and the Committee shall give all parties concerned an opportunity to be heard and to present witnesses and evidence. The Committee may call for additional evidence from other qualified persons present at the event. After hearing all of the evidence the Committee shall consider the matter and shall, if possible, reach an immediate decision and inform the persons involved.

3. A report of the meeting, giving all of the essential evidence and the Committee's decision, together with the original written protest and the $25.00 deposit if not refunded, must be mailed to The American Kennel Club postmarked within nine (9) days after completion of the event.

4. An appeal to The American Kennel Club from a decision of a Committee on any such protest, may be made by either the owner of the hound protested or the person who made the protest. The appeal must be received by The American Kennel Club within thirty (30) days after the date of the Committee's decision.

SECTION 2. PROTESTING THE LURE FIELD TRIAL OR TEST. Any member of a club licensed to hold a Lure Field Trial or Test, or any participant in the Lure Field Trial or Test may lodge a "protest of proceedings" should he/she desire to do so. The following procedure must be followed:

1. A written statement lodging the protest, and explicitly describing the infringement or irregular procedure or ruling, accompanied by a twenty-five dollar ($25.00) protest filing fee (when paying by check, the check should be made out to The American Kennel Club) is given to the Field Chairman during the trial or test hours.

2. The Field Committee must make a ruling in writing as soon as possible, a copy of which shall be given to the protestor, on that day.

3. All monies, copies of the protest and copies of the Field Committee rulings must be mailed to the AKC and be postmarked within nine (9) days of the trial.

4. If an appeal of the decision of the Field Committee is desired, an additional letter from the protestor must be received by The American Kennel Club postmarked within nine (9) days of the trial.

The letter must specify the basis of the protest and the reason for the appeal.

5. Protests upheld may result in action deemed appropriate by The American Kennel Club.

    a. Protests upheld are cause for reimbursement of the $25.00 filing fee to the protesting individual.

    b. Protests not upheld cause forfeit of the $25.00 filing fee to The American Kennel Club.

6. In all cases, the individual protesting is informed of the ruling on the protest appeal within sixty (60) days of the date of the trial.

SECTION 3. STATEMENTS OF IRREGULARITIES. Statements of irregularities must be sent to the AKC within thirty (30) days of the trial.

Chapter XV
Disqualification and Reinstatement of Hounds

SECTION 1. DISQUALIFICATION.

1. A hound's privilege to participate will be immediately withdrawn upon a disqualification.

2. A hound's privilege to participate will be immediately withdrawn if it is dismissed twice within six (6) trials.

3. The AKC will inform, in writing, the individual or individuals whose hound was disqualified, and cite the reason given for the hound's disqualification. (See Chapter IV, Sections 10 and 11.)

SECTION 2. REINSTATEMENT. The privilege to participate may be reinstated upon completion of:

1. a minimum of a calendar month of retraining as appropriate,

2. certification in writing by two (2) Judges stating the hound is running cleanly, with two other hounds of the same breed,

3. a letter and the certifications sent to The American Kennel Club from the owner of the hound applying for reinstatement, and

4. a decision by the AKC to reinstate said privilege.

A hound disqualified a second time is not eligible for reinstatement.

Lure Field Trials—Glossary of Terms

Blanket:

A colorful cloth worn by the hounds during a course. At present the colors being used are yellow, pink and blue.

Course:

Consists of 1, 2 or 3 hounds pursuing a lure of either mechanical or electrical drive over a selected course pattern. The course begins after the handlers' affirmative response to "Are you ready?" and ends when all hounds in the course are under handlers' physical restraint.

Course Delay:

A course delay shall include delays caused by hounds whose handlers delay the start of the course, hounds that break away from and avoid their handlers prior to the request "Are you ready?" and hounds that avoid their handlers after the command, "Retrieve your hounds."

Draw:

A random drawing determining the order in which the hounds will run.

Household:

Includes those persons that comprise a unit living together in the same shared dwelling.

Immediate Family:

Includes siblings, parents, grandparents, spouse and children.

Pre-Slip:

Where a hound is slipped before the Tally-Ho is sounded by the Huntmaster.

Qualifying Score:

50% of the total possible combined points from the preliminary and final courses.

Dog Show; and "Lure Coursing Trial regulations" any as advanced and/or from any Secretary at trial where they are officiating or from

THE AMERICAN KENNEL CLUB, 51 MADISON AVENUE, NEW YORK, NY 10010

AGREEMENT

I (we) acknowledge that the "Rules Applying to Registration and Dog Shows" and, if this entry is for a lure coursing trial, the "Lure Coursing Trial regulations" have been made available to me (us), and that I (we/we are) (familiar with their contents. I (we) agree that the club holding this trial has the right to refuse this entry (or cause which the club shall deem to be sufficient. In consideration of the acceptance of this entry and of the holding of the trial and of the opportunity to have the hound judged and to win prize money, ribbons, or trophies. I (we) agree to hold this club, its members, directors, governors, officers, agents, superintendents or show secretary and the owner or lessor of the premises and any employees of the aforementioned parties, harmless from any claim for loss or injury which may be alleged to have been caused directly or indirectly to any person or thing by the act of this dog while in or upon the show or trial premises or grounds or near any entrance thereto, and I (we) personally assume all responsibility and liability for any such claim; and I (we) further agree to hold the aforementioned parties harmless for damage or injury to the dog, whether such loss, disappearance, theft, damage or injury, be caused or alleged to be caused by the negligence of the club or any of the parties aforementioned, or by the negligence of any other person, or any other cause or cause.

I (we) hereby assume the sole responsibility for and agree to indemnify and save the aforementioned parties harmless from any and all loss and expense (including legal (fees) by reason of the liability imposed by law upon any of the aforementioned parties for damage because of bodily injuries, including death at any time resulting therefrom, sustained by any person or persons, including myself (ourselves) or on account of damage to property, arising out of or in consequence of my (our) participation in this trial, however such injuries, death or damage to property may be caused, and whether or not the same may have been caused or may be alleged to have been caused by negligence of the aforementioned parties or any of their employees or agents, or any other persons.

INSTRUCTION

A dog must be entered in the name of the person who actually owned it at the time entries for a trial closed. If a registered dog has been acquired by a new owner, it must be entered in the name of its new owner in any trial for which entries closed after the date of acquirement, regardless of whether the new owner has received the registration certificate indicating that the dog is recorded in his name. State an entry form whether transfer application has been mailed to A.C.C. (For complete rule refer to Chapter 14, Section 3 of the AKC Rules Applying to Registration And Dog Show.)

☐ Please separate my entries.

Club: _____ Date: _____

Secretary/Address: _____

Entry Fees: I enclose $ _____ for entry fees.

Entry For: ☐ JC Test ☐ SC Test ☐ Open ☐ Hound DISMISSED within last 6 Trials.

CALL NAME: Sequence # to be assigned by the Trial Secretary: _____

Breed: _____ Date of Birth: _____ Sex: ☐ Dog ☐ Bitch

Registered Name: _____

Breeder: _____

Enter number here

☐ AKC REG NO. _____ Sire: _____

☐ ILP NO. _____

☐ FOREIGN REG NO. & COUNTRY _____ Dam: _____

Actual Owner(s): _____ ☐ Ownership Change

Owner's Address: _____ ☐ Change of Address

City: _____ State: _____ Zip: _____

Name of Owner's Agent (if any) at Trial: _____

I CERTIFY that I am the actual owner of the hound, or that I am the duly authorized agent of the actual owner whose name I have entered above. In consideration of the acceptance of this entry. I (we) agree to abide by the rules and regulations of The American Kennel Club in effect at the time of this trial, an by any additional rules and regulations appearing in the premium list for this trial, and further agree to be bound by the Agreement printed on the reverse side of this entry form. I (we) certify and represent that the dog entered in not a hazard to persons or other dogs. This entry is submitted for acceptance on the foregoing representation and agreement.

Signature of owner or his agent duly authorized to make this entry: _____

Telephone: ( ) _____

☐ Please separate my entries.

Front and back of official American Kennel Club lure coursing entry form.

101

Run-Off:
A competition to determine a final placement.

Clubs

All American Sighthound Field Association Member and Affiliate Clubs prior to July 1, 1992, are eligible to apply to The American Kennel Club for approval to hold a Lure Coursing Trial and/or Test.

Any American Sighthound Field Association Club that is also a Member Club of The American Kennel Club will be licensed to hold AKC Member Lure Coursing Trials and/or Tests, subject to AKC approval.

After July 1, 1992, applicant Clubs must follow American Kennel Club procedures. Write to the AKC (51 Madison Avenue, New York, NY 10010) for an application form and qualifications to become a licensed club.

Judges

Qualified American Sighthound Field Association Judges, prior to July 1, 1992, are eligible to apply to The American Kennel Club for approval to judge at AKC Lure Coursing Trials and Tests.

After July 1, 1992, applicants for judging must follow the American Kennel Club procedures.

Write to AKC (51 Madison Avenue, New York, NY 10010) for an application form and qualifications to be listed on AKC Approved Judges list.

AMERICAN SIGHTHOUND FIELD ASSOCIATION RUNNING RULES AND FIELD PROCEDURES FOR LURE FIELD TRIALS

Statement of Purpose

The American Sighthound Field Association is an organization of sighthound fanciers dedicated to the common goal of preserving and further developing the natural beauty, grace, speed and coursing skill of the sighthound. We will endeavor to promote a recognized system of Lure Field Trials for sighthounds throughout the United States, governed by rules that can be accepted by the American Kennel Club.

CHAPTER I
General Rules

Section 1. Only purebred Afghan Hounds, Basenjis, Borzois, Greyhounds, Ibizan Hounds, Irish Wolfhounds, Pharaoh Hounds, Rhodesian Ridgebacks, Salukis, Scottish Deerhounds and Whippets may be entered in Lure Field Trials. All hounds must be not less than one year old on the day of the trial. All entries shall be individually registered with the American Kennel Club, the National Greyhound Association, an American Kennel Club recognized foreign registry, or possess a Critique Case Number from the Saluki Club of America. The owner of a hound is required to notify the Records Coordinator of any change in registration number.

Section 2. The owner or agent entering a hound in a Lure Field Trial does so at his own risk. The owner or agent and licensed club agree to abide by the rules of the ASFA and the American Kennel Club.

Section 3. Entry fees shall be fixed by the Host Club and shall be forfeited in such cases where hounds are scratched from the field for causes.

(a) Hounds determined to have a breed disqualification at the time of Roll Call shall be barred from competition and their entry fees shall be refunded. Spayed, monorchid, cryptorchid, and neutered hounds without breed disqualifications may be entered.

(b) Hounds determined to be lame at the time of Roll Call shall be barred from competition and their entry fees shall be refunded.

(c) Bitches in season, or which come in season after the close of entries, shall be expected from this rule and their entry fees shall be refunded. Notification to the Field Secretary of bitches in season must be made before or during the Roll Call. Bitches known to be in season should not be brought onto the trial grounds.

Section 4. There shall be no consumption of any type of alcoholic beverages or illegal drugs by any Judge, by any member of the Field Committee, or by anyone working in any official capacity prior to the completion of their assignment. Said consumption shall be deemed detrimental to the sport of Lure Field Trials.

Section 5. The Board of Directors shall have authority to issue, from time to time, where necessary, notices that amplify, clarify or interpret these running rules. These notices shall become effective on a specific date following distribution to all clubs and shall remain in effect unless revised by the Annual Convention of Delegates.

CHAPTER II

Officials

All Lure Field Trials shall have the following officials: Field Committee and Judge(s). The names of these officials shall appear on the club's Premium List. The Field Committee shall consist of no less than 5 individuals who shall fill the positions of: Field Secretary, Field Chairman, Field Clerk, Huntmaster, Lure Operator and Inspection Committee. They shall be responsible for the following duties which may be delegated as appropriate.

Section 1. Field Secretary (must be a member of the Host Club)

1. Is a member of the Field Committee.
2. Applies for a date to hold a sanctioned Lure Field Trial.
3. Solicits in writing and receives in writing confirmation of Judging assignments prior to submitting the Premium List for approval, a copy of which shall be made available to the ASFA Corresponding Secretary upon request.
4. Prepares and mails out premium lists and entry forms after receiving official approval and accepts entries. If not stated in the Premium List, Field Secretaries shall notify, at the same time as they verify the entry, the entrant of approximate time of roll call for the stake entered.
5. Any Field Secretary or Host Club which accepts an entry fee other than that published in its Premium List or entry form, or in any way discriminates between entrants, shall be disciplined. All persons found guilty of paying or receiving any monies, special inducements or allowances in violation of the foregoing shall be disciplined.
6. The Field Secretary may decline any entries for cause for a period limited to 12 months from the first refusal of entry for cause, but each instance the Secretary shall file good and sufficient reasons for so doing with the Corresponding Secretary of the ASFA.

7. The Field Secretary shall decline any late, incomplete, unsigned, unpaid or conditional entries. Each entry must be completed in full and the information given on the form must be that which applies to that entered hound. The entry form must be signed by the owner or agent duly authorized to make the entry.
8. Provides the Field Chairman with a list of hounds entered.
9. Shall have available for each and every member of the Field Committee, and any and all other officials, copies of the latest updated edition of this book.
10. Insures that all records are collected and forwarded with per-capita fees to reach the ASFA Records Coordinator within 14 days or be postmarked within 10 days of the meet.

Section 2. Field Chairman (must be a member of the Host Club)

1. Is chairman of the Field Committee.
2. Provides the grounds for the meet.
3. Shall appoint an inspection committee who shall have the responsibility of inspecting all hounds entered. (See Sec. 6, ''Inspection Committee,'' this Chapter.)
4. Carries out, before the official draw, a Roll Call of entered hounds. Hounds not present shall be scratched.
5. Insures that all equipment is in place and functioning, including:
   (a) Proper color and size blankets.
   (b) All record sheets and Judges' scoring sheets.
6. Insures that all placement awards are on hand.
7. Provides for ''policing,'' i.e., clean-up of the grounds before, during and after the meet, especially of anything remotely resembling a lure and anything hazardous.
8. Must individually approve anyone who is to be allowed in the judging area other than the Officials of the trial (e.g., apprentice Judges).
9. May, at his discretion, excuse from the field for the day any hound that exhibits uncontrolled aggressive behavior toward any person or hound on the trial grounds, except hounds competing in the course then in progress. The Field Chairman may also excuse, or levy and collect a penalty fee of $5 from the owner or his duly authorized agent of any hound that is loose on the field and not in competition at the time.
10. In the event of an Official Protest, the Field Chairman shall notify the Judges immediately.

Section 3. Field Clerk

1. Is a member of the Field Committee.
2. Is responsible for the draw of hounds in competition.
3. Shall be stationed on the field and shall promptly collect the score sheets from the Judges upon the completion of the judging of each course.
4. Keeps score on the Record Sheets including Judges' scores per hound. The Field Clerk shall notify the Judge of any arithmetic or blanket color errors on the Judges Sheets, and said error shall be corrected and initialed by the Judge. The Field Clerk shall not change any Judge's scores (see Ch. III, Sec. 17).
5. Posts preliminary scores of each breed before finals, final scores before run-offs and Best of Breed runs and Best of Breed scores before Best in Field runs.
6. Shall announce the final placements and scores at the end of the stake or trial.

Section 4. Huntmaster

1. Is a member of the Field Committee.
2. Will be in complete charge of all hounds and handlers (see also Ch. V, Sec. 12).
3. Shall call up each new course as each previous course is completed.
4. Will insure that a handler handles but one hound in each course.
5. Must explain release and retrieval procedures before each preliminary course only.
6. Shall stand in close proximity to, but not in front of, the handlers and hounds.
7. The lure must be positioned in front of the hounds and in the direction in which it will travel before the signal is given to activate it. The lure shall not be brought up from behind the hounds.
8. As the Huntmaster is facing the lure, the hounds shall be placed as follows: YELLOW on the left, PINK in the middle or to the right in braces, BLUE on the right in trios.
9. Shall not tease the hounds with the lure.
10. Shall question, in the following order, the Judge(s), Lure Operator and handlers ''Are you ready?'' and after affirmative answers, the course is begun for the purposes of determining a pre-slip.

11. Provides a hand signal to the Lure Operator to start the lure.
12. Gives the signal "Tally-Ho" to release the hounds for each course, and "Retrieve your Hounds" when appropriate.
13. Hounds should not be slipped before the sound of the "T" in "Tally-Ho." Will notify the handler of the pre-slipped hound and the Judge(s) of any pre-slips immediately at the end of each course. If the Huntmaster fails to notify the Judge(s) of a pre-slip, then to all intents there has been no pre-slip, but the Judge(s) shall have the prerogative to question the Huntmaster at any time if the release seems questionable.
14. Will cause the lure to be stopped upon a pre-slip and restart provided no Tally-Ho has been sounded.
15. Will inspect the lure before every course and replace it if needed.
16. Will neither pick up nor authorize anyone to pick up or touch the lure until such time as all hounds are on lead and moving away from the finish line, unless the lure is lying on the ground in the clear.
17. Insures that the lure be restrung immediately upon completion of each course.
18. Shall notify the Inspection Committee if any of the hounds appears lame.
19. Shall inform immediately the handlers of all hounds in a course that is called a no-course or a course in which a dog is dismissed or disqualified.

Section 5. Lure Operator
1. Is a member of the Field Committee.
2. Will lay out the course according to the approved course plan.
3. Will make at least one pilot run of the lure before the first course of the day and upon reversing or changing the course layout.
4. Starts the lure at the signal from the Huntmaster and stops it at least 20 yards before the lure machine if possible.
5. Will attempt to keep the lure 10 to 30 yards in front of the lead hound at all times after the course begins. (See Ch. III, Sec. 6.) In the event a hound becomes unsighted, the lure must continue in the originally planned direction until completion of the course.
6. Will stop the lure on a signal from the Huntmaster or Judge(s), but shall automatically stop the lure any time a hound becomes entangled in the string or when a potentially dangerous situation may develop.
7. Shall not operate the lure for any stake where any hound which he

owns or co-owns or is co-owned by a member of his immediate family or residence is entered.

8. The same Lure Operator shall operate the lure throughout an entire stake.

Section 6. Inspection Committee

1. Are members of the Field Committee.
2. The Inspection Committee shall consist of three people whose duties shall be to inspect each entry for lameness, bitches in season, and breed disqualifications, at Roll Call. The Inspection Committee shall also investigate and report its findings to the Field Chairman regarding any observed or reported aggressiveness of any hound or abuse or mistreatment of any hound on the grounds during the trial hours.
3. Any hound found to have a breed disqualification, to be lame, or any bitch in season shall be barred from competition and entry fees shall be refunded by check within 90 days of the trial. This measurement and determination of breed disqualifications shall be the responsibility of the Inspection Committee.
4. If a hound is injured in the meet or becomes lame in the meet, the Inspection Committee shall determine whether the hound may continue to compete or whether it shall be withdrawn. A hound so withdrawn shall not be entitled to a refund of its entry fee.
5. The procedure for measuring is as follows:

(a) The hound being measured shall be placed on a flat, level surface that is not slippery. The handler shall position the hound at the Inspection Committee's discretion. The hound shall be in a naturally alert position, with the head up but not stretched upward, and with its feet well under it and its forelegs vertical as viewed both from the front and side.

(b) A member of the Inspection Committee, of which there shall be three members, shall first determine the highest point over the shoulder blades with one hand, and shall then pass the measuring wicket over the hound from the rear with the other hand, and place the wicket so the cross piece comes down directly on the highest point over the shoulder blades. The wicket should not be placed on the neck in front of the shoulder or on the spinal column behind the shoulder blades. At least two members of the Inspection Committee must agree that a hound is within or outside the height limits.

(c) All hounds will be measured only once and at the time of

Roll Call at each and every Field Trial with the exception that hounds that have been awarded the F. Ch. title shall not be measured unless such measurement is requested by an exhibitor, Judge, or the Field Committee.

(d) Handlers will be allowed only two minutes to position their dogs in a proper standing position. Hounds that cannot be made to stand in the proper position for measurement on two attempts will not be allowed to course, and their entry fees will be forfeited.

Section 7. Field Committee

1. The Field Committee will make every attempt to conduct the trial in accordance with what is published in the Premium List. Changes may only be made out of necessity, not convenience. This includes the Field Committee and their assignments, Judges, Lure Operators, and course plan.
2. Field Committees may make such general regulations or additional rules for the government of their Field Trials as shall be considered necessary and proper, provided such regulations or rules do not conflict with, change or modify any running rule or field procedure of the ASFA. Such additional regulations or rules shall be printed and distributed with the Premium List and violations thereof shall be considered the same as violations of the rules and regulations of the ASFA.
3. The decision of the Field Committee shall be final, conclusive and binding on all parties, in all matters occurring on the day of the meet, except for matters coming within the jurisdiction of the Judge(s), but such Committee decisions must be made in accord with the general running rules and standard procedures that apply to the trial being held. All decisions are subject to the rules of the ASFA.
4. If it becomes necessary to replace a published Judge after the opening of the Lure Field Trial and no person on the eligible judges list is available to take the aforementioned Judge's place, the Field Committee may select as a substitute for the published Judge a person whose name is not on the eligible judges list provided such person is not currently suspended from the privileges of the ASFA. The Field Committee must announce the name of any substitute Judge before the draw for the stake at which he is to officiate.

5. In the case where a Judge is unable to complete his judging assignment a replacement may be substituted. The Field Committee shall notify the exhibitors of the substitution. All of the scores of the Judge that was replaced shall stand as recorded.
6. If a Judge is substituted in a stake in which an owner has a hound entered, he has the option of withdrawing his hound before the draw and receiving his entry fee back. If, subsequent to the draw, a Judge must be substituted, no refunds shall be made.
7. In the event a published Lure Operator cannot fulfill his assignment, the Field Committee must select a substitute Lure Operator and must announce the name of that substitute before the draw for the stake at which he is to operate the lure. If a Lure Operator is substituted in a stake in which an owner has a hound entered, he has the option of withdrawing his hound before the draw and receiving his entry fee back. If, subsequent to the draw, a Lure Operator must be substituted, no refunds shall be made. The published Lure Operator shall make every effort to complete his assignment.
8. The Field Committee shall handle all official protests on the day of the Lure Field Trial as specified in Ch. IX.

CHAPTER III
Judging

In addition to those rules and procedures set forth in Chapter II, as they relate to Judges, the following shall apply:

Section 1. Clubs may, at their discretion, use either one or two Judges for any given breed or breeds at ASFA Lure Field Trials. If only one Judge is used, he or she must be regularly licensed for each breed so judged.

Section 2. A person shall not judge the same breed or breeds ALONE on two consecutive days within a 150-mile radius.

Section 3. No Judge shall handle a hound in the stake or stakes where he is officiating, nor shall a hound belonging to any Judge or his immediate family or residence be entered in any stake where that Judge is officiating. Such hounds may be entered at that meet in other stakes where the Judge is not officiating.

Section 4. Each and every Judge, before beginning his assignment, shall walk the course and verify with the Field Chairman that an approved course plan is properly staked.

Section 5. While on the field during his judging assignment, no Judge shall discuss anything relative to his judging assignment with any handler or agent.

Section 6. While observing the course in progress, when two Judges are used, the Judges shall stand apart. They shall not converse during the running of the course, nor shall they discuss anything pertaining to that course, except to state "no course," until the score sheets have been turned in to the Field Clerk or his representative.

Section 7. A Judge shall be able to call a no-course at any time:

(a) the hounds are interfered with or disrupted or he cannot fairly score the course.

(b) when a segment of the lure falls off and any hound reacts to said segment, but only if he cannot fairly score the course.

(c) If a hound or hounds touch or catch the lure and, in the Judge's(s') opinion(s), by so doing that action causes interference with the running of the course, it shall be declared a no-course. Any time a hound becomes entangled in the string, the Judge(s) shall order the lure stopped and may declare a no-course.

(d) If the Lure Operator fails to maintain the 10–30 yard limit, and the hounds become unsighted, a Judge shall have the prerogative to call a no-course. If either Judge calls a no-course on one or more of the hounds in a course, both Judges will score the re-course.

Section 8. Judges are responsible for scoring all categories in all courses: preliminaries, finals, run-offs, etc.

Section 9. Placing of winners shall be decided on the basis of qualities evidenced by: enthusiasm, follow, speed, agility and endurance in scoring the hounds. Judges shall score in whole numbers only, and shall be governed by the following system:

Enthusiasm .... 15 pts.

Follow .... 15 pts.

Speed .... 25 pts.

Agility .... 25 pts.

Endurance .... 20 pts.

.... Total: 100 pts.

Less: Pre-slip penalty .... − 1 to − 10 pts.
    (from each Judge). When a pre-slip occurs, each Judge shall levy

a penalty of between 1 and 10 points for that course. The pre-slip penalty shall not be carried over in the case where a no-course is called on the course in progress.

Less: Course delay penalty .... − 1 to − 10 pts. (from each Judge). When a course delay occurs, each Judge shall levy a 1 to 10 point penalty for that course. The course delay penalty shall be carried over in the case where a no-course is called on the course in progress and shall be cumulative in the case of repeated delays.

Section 10. A Judge may score some hounds in a course and rerun other hounds from the same course. At their discretion, the Judge may score hounds which fail to complete the course for any reason, if a Judge is able to do so. In the case where the hounds fail to run in the preliminary course, a Judge shall have the option of giving the hounds a minimum score or excusing them.

Section 11. A zero total score from both Judges, or a Judge when only one is used, in the preliminary course automatically excuses a hound for the day. The hound shall be considered as having been in competition when computing points, if scored in the preliminary course.

Section 12. Hounds may be excused from the field by a Judge for the following reasons:

(a) Hounds who fail to run after the Tally-Ho in either the preliminary or final course.
(b) Hounds who may be considered unfit to compete.
(c) Hounds who course other hounds rather than the lure.
(d) Hounds whose handlers or owners interfere with the Judges or officials.
(e) Hounds who delay the course.
(f) Handlers who willfully interfere with another competitor, his hound or any official.

Section 13. Hounds shall be dismissed from the field by a Judge, for the day, for interfering (aggressively or playfully) with the course of another hound. (Growling and/or barking, in and of itself, does not constitute grounds for dismissal.)

Section 14. Hounds shall be disqualified by the Judge, or by agreement of both Judges where two are used, for the following reason: Fighting—the aggressor in fighting in the field. In the event that only one of two Judges disqualifies a hound, this disqualification constitutes a dismissal.

Section 15. If a hound is excused, dismissed or disqualified, the course may be called a no-course by a Judge. The remaining hound or hounds may be run in a remaining course if one exists or be given the opportunity to re-run alone and be scored.

Section 16. Judges shall immediately inform the Huntmaster when a course is called a no-course or when a hound is dismissed or disqualified (see Ch. II, Sec. 4, #19).

Section 17. Judges must state on the Judges Sheet the specific reason for excusal, dismissal or disqualification.

Section 18. After a course has been judged, and the marked score sheets turned over to the Field Clerk, only the Judge can change his final score and only in the case of an arithmetical or blanket color error.

Section 19. The Judge's decisions upon all matters relating to the course are final and binding. The Board of Directors of the ASFA may reverse, change or modify a Judge's decision, but only in accordance with the procedures in Chapter IX.

CHAPTER IV
Scheduling the Meet

Section 1. An approved date must be obtained for a Lure Field Trial. The requesting club must be sanctioned by the American Sighthound Field Association. Applications for dates must be submitted in writing to the Scheduling Committee; such applications must be submitted by the Field Secretary or an authorized member of the host club at least 45 days prior to the date requested. Requests for dates shall include:

  (a) Name of Host Club.
  (b) Date(s) requested.
  (c) Location of trial.
  (d) All-breed or specialty trial.

Section 2. The sanction to hold a Lure Field Trial is granted for a specified time period. The Host Club does not have the option of completing a trial at a future date or at another locale, except in the case of an extreme act of nature or a catastrophe. Under such circumstances the affected club will submit written substantiation to the ASFA Board of Directors for review.

Section 3. Two sample copies of the Premium List and entry form must be sent to the Scheduling Committee and one sample copy to the President of the ASFA no less than 45 days prior to the approved date. A Field Secretary may not mail out the Premium List until such time as it has been approved for mailing by the Scheduling Committee.

If a club wishes to hold a trial on their priority date, they must request this from the Scheduling Chair in writing at least 120 days before the date of the trial.

1. Premium Lists must be 5½ inches wide and 8½ inches high. The entry form and premium must be of the same size and must conform exactly to the list of requirements included in this Chapter.
2. Closing date, limitations of entries and entry fees are left to the discretion of the Host Club.
3. A final copy of the approved Premium List must be sent to the Scheduling Committee and to the Regional Director of that area in advance of the trial date.
4. Each trial shall have a separate Premium List.
5. Only information pertaining to that trial shall be included on the Premium List. (Separate enclosures mailed with the Premium List are acceptable.)
6. Exhibition Only Stakes are not considered part of the Trial, and shall not be included in the Premium List.
7. All-Breed Trials on the same date will be 150 miles or more apart.
8. A club or association that has held a trial or trials in any one year shall have first right to claim the corresponding date(s) for its trial(s) to be held in the next succeeding year.

   If a club wishes to hold a Trial on their priority date, they must request this from the Scheduling Chair, in writing, at least 120 days before the date of the Trial.

Section 4. Only those persons whose names appear on the List of Eligible Judges of the ASFA, which shall be published from time to time in the *Field Advisory News*, may, in the discretion of the Association, be approved to judge at any sanctioned Lure Field Trial.

Section 5. Course Plans. Exact layouts, including approximate distances between turns, and locations of hills, gullies, fences, etc., of proposed coursing plans must be in the Premium List.

1. No course shall be less than 500 yards. It is recommended that a course be no less than 600 yards whenever possible.
2. When using a continuous loop system every attempt shall be made when laying out the course plan to assure that the lure does not traverse the course twice in order to meet the distance requirements. The minimum distance of line used on the continuous loop shall be 500 yards.
3. When using a continuous loop system, mid-course reversals are permissible so long as they are clearly stated in the Premium List and provided that the place and duration of the reversal is the same or approximately the same for each and every course.

Section 6. Entry Forms. Entry forms must include: name of Host Club, date of trial, Field Secretary's name and address, closing date(s) of entries, and entry fee(s).

Section 7. Required Contents of Premium Lists

1. Each Premium List must contain all of the items enumerated in this list.

Front Cover
    (a) Closing date(s) for entries and entry limits (if any).
    (b) Club name (logo optional).
    (c) All-breed or single breed trial.
    (d) Date of trial.
    (e) Location of trial (street, town and state).
    (f) Entry fee(s).
    (g) "Permission has been granted by the American Sighthound Field Association for the holding of this event under American Sighthound Field Association Rules and Regulations. .... , Chairman, ASFA Scheduling Committee."

First Page (inside front cover)
    (h) Club officers and directors.
    (i) Judges and their complete addresses and assignments. (An asterisk shall be used to denote Provisional status.)
    (j) Field Committee, including Chairman, Secretary, Field Clerk, Lure Operator, Huntmaster and Inspection Committee.
    (k) Ribbon prizes; color for placements 1st through NBQ, Best of Breed and Best in Field (if offered).

(l) Trial hours.

(m) Roll call(s).

(n) Entries will (or will not) be acknowledged by mail (or telephone).

(o) Breed or list of breeds eligible to enter, ''Only purebred Afghan Hounds, Basenjis, Borzois, Greyhounds, Ibizan Hounds, Irish Wolfhounds, Pharaoh Hounds, Salukis, Scottish Deerhounds and Whippets may be entered.''

(p) ''All entries shall be individually registered with the American Kennel Club, the National Greyhound Association, or an American Kennel Club–recognized foreign registry, or possess a Critique Case Number from the Saluki Club of America.''

Second Page (inside back cover)

(q) Stakes offered. Regular stakes must be listed: *Open Stake*, any eligible sighthound excluding Field Champions of record; *Field Champion Stake*, any ASFA Field Champion. *Singles stake*—optional. Best in Field will or will not be offered. (Non-regular Stakes: Breeder, Kennel and Veteran—optional.)

(r) All entries must be one year of age or older on the day of the trial.

(s) Stake will (or will not) be split if the entry in any one stake is 24 or more at the time of the draw.

(t) All hounds will run twice, in trios if possible, or braces, unless excused, dismissed or disqualified.

(u) Bitches in season and lame hounds will be excused.

(v) Hounds not present at the time of Roll Call will be scratched.

(w) Type of lure machine. (Examples: battery-powered take-up reel; or battery-powered continuous loop system.)

(x) Type of lure. (Examples: highly visible plastic strips; or a combination of highly visible plastic and fur; or fur.)

(y) Course plan. A diagram to approximate scale, including total number of yards, obstacles (if any) and distances between pulleys. Also must include indication of the start and finish of the course and whether it will (or will not) be reversed for final courses. (Description of grounds/terrain—as needed.)

2. The following optional information may be included in Premium Lists:

(a) Veterinary care.

(b) Equipment available (slipleads, blankets, etc.).

(c) Food and/or water for handlers and/or hounds.

(d) Trophies.

(e) If muzzles are required it must be so stated; otherwise, optional.

(f) If substitutions for hounds are allowed after the closing date this must be stated in the Premium List.

(g) "The club reserves the right to alter the course diagram as required by weather and/or field conditions on the day of the trial," included with the course plan.

(h) Return address and/or directions to the trial site.

(i) Reasonable health restrictions.

(j) General information on *Field Advisory News*.

CHAPTER V
Running the Meet

Section 1. At a breed-only trial two regular stakes shall be offered, i.e., Open and Field Champion; at an all-breed trial two regular stakes shall be offered in all breeds, i.e., Open and Field Champion. The Host Club may offer a single-breed only or, at its option, an all-breed trial.

Section 2. No hound may be entered in more than one regular stake at a meet.

Section 3. The Judge or Judges must be the same for all stakes in any one breed, unless a Judge is unable to complete his assignment (see Ch. II, Sec. 7, #3 & 4).

Section 4. Regular stakes are described as follows:

(a) OPEN STAKE: Each stake shall consist of entries of only one breed, dogs and bitches; Field Champions of record of that breed may not be entered.

(b) FIELD CHAMPION STAKE: Each stake shall consist of entries of only one breed, dogs and bitches, who are Field Champions of record. Hounds whose owners' records show them to be Field Champions may be entered for a period up to 90 days without official certification.

Hounds whose owners' records show them to have met the requirements for the Field Champion title may be changed from the Open Stake to the Field Champion Stake provided notification is made to the Field Secretary prior to roll call.

(c) NOVICE STAKE: Permitted at Fun Lure Trials only (see the Novice Stake Guidelines in the Appendix).

Section 5. The following description applies to all regular stakes:

(a) At the option of the Host Club, when the entry in any regular stake at the time of the draw reaches 20 or more, the stake may be divided as evenly as possible. There should be a minimum of 10 in each stake.

(b) Every entry in the regular stakes, not excused, dismissed or disqualified, shall be run twice. The order of running for both courses shall be by random draw. (See Chap. V, Sec. 7.)

(c) Hounds absent at Roll Call or at the running of their stake shall be scratched.

(d) After completion and posting of final scores, all hounds no longer required for further judging are excused.

(e) The top five placing hounds in each stake shall be determined by the combined scores of the preliminary and final runs.

(f) ASFA points are awarded to the first through fourth placements in all regular stakes.

(g) Ties for the top five placements in any stake will be run off or forfeited. If one hound in a tie runoff is dismissed or disqualified, the hound not dismissed or disqualified is considered to have won the runoff.

(h) All hounds entered in a given stake shall be divided into trios, if possible, or braces. Hounds shall be designated by colors according to their drawing.

1st number drawn .... Bright YELLOW
(placed on the left)

2nd number drawn .... Bright PINK
(middle or on the right in braces)

3rd number drawn .... Bright BLUE
(placed on the right)

Section 6. First placing hounds in all stakes of each breed shall run off or withdraw from Best of Breed competition. Unless all ties for first place and Best of Breed can be resolved in one course, all ties must be broken before running Best of Breed. If only three hounds are involved, the tie should be broken with the Best of Breed run. The winner of this run or the remaining hound shall be declared that breed's Best of Breed. Only hounds winning a Best of Breed run shall be awarded points equal to the points awarded the highest placing hound in that breed which it defeated. In the event of a single entry in any breed, or all hounds in a breed entered in one stake, the Best of Breed winner shall be determined solely by the highest combined scores of the preliminary and final courses. A hound must earn a qualifying score in the runoff in order to win Best of Breed.

A hound excused, dismissed or disqualified in a runoff and/or Best of Breed run shall not lose prior points or placements earned that day. A dismissal or disqualification in a runoff and/or Best of Breed run shall count on the hound's record in accordance with Chapter VIII, 'Disqualification and Reinstatement of Hounds.'

Section 7. Conducting the Draw

1. Each hound shall be assigned a number and the order and arrangement of hounds coursing shall be determined by a random drawing of those numbers by breed at the beginning of the Field Trial or stake.
2. The draw shall be after the Roll Call on the day of the trial, and shall be made in full public view on the trial grounds. This applies to all drawings of all regular and non-regular stakes.
3. Upon request from an owner or owner's agent at Roll Call, multiple entries from an owner shall be divided as evenly as possible between the stakes (if split) and (or) each course if the stake is not split. This does not apply to the Best in Field competition. In the event of a Kennel Stake, the separation shall divide the Kennel entry.
4. When there is but a single course in a regular stake in which an owner or his duly authorized agent has more than one hound, these hounds will be run together or one or more will be scratched by owner or his duly authorized agent, without refund of entry fee.
5. If only one member of a breed is entered, that hound may be run with another breed if all exhibitors involved agree. The hounds would be scored separately.
6. A single entry in a stake may be drawn to run with any other stake of that breed if all the handlers involved agree. The hounds would be scored separately. The Judges shall not be informed which courses are combined.

7. A hound that has received a minimum score of less than half the total possible points in the preliminary course shall be eligible to compete in the final course. A hound that is excused will not be permitted to run in the final course, and will not be counted as having been in competition when computing the points.
8. After the draw is completed should, for any reason, a hound fail to appear for its course, such that a single hound remains to be run, that remaining hound will be run and scored alone, unless that hound can be added to a brace, should one exist, in a preceding or subsequent course.

Section 8. Singles Stake

At the option of the Host Club a Singles Stake may be offered. If the Host Club offers this stake, it must so state in the Premium List. All rules pertaining to Regular Stakes shall apply except when inconsistent with the following:

(a) Each hound shall run the course alone.

(b) No ASFA points or placements towards a Field Championship or an LCM shall be awarded.

(c) Placements shall be awarded based on the combined Preliminary and Final course scores only. The winner of this stake shall not be eligible to compete in Best of Breed and/or Best in Field courses.

(d) When the Singles Stake entry in any one breed is four or less, these breeds shall be combined into a Mixed Singles Stake. Breeds with five or more entries in the Singles Stake shall be judged as a Singles Breed Stake.

(e) Only hounds found lame or in season at Roll Call shall be barred from competition in this stake.

(f) A hound entered in the Singles Stake shall not be eligible to enter the Open and/or Field Champion Stake at that trial.

(g) The Host Club may place a limit on the Singles Stake entry separate from any limit placed on entries at the trial.

Section 9. Best in Field

At the option of the Host Club a Best in Field may be offered. All Best of Breed winners shall be eligible to compete in the Best in Field competition. If the Host Club offers this competition, it must so indicate in the Premium List.

(a) The order of running is to be determined by random draw.

(b) Multiple entries from one owner will not be split into separate courses, if drawn together.

120

(c) There will be only one run.

(d) No ASFA championship points will be awarded; however, the hound that wins Best in Field will be credited with a first placement in a stake.

(e) The highest scoring hound will be declared the Best in Field on that day.

(f) An excusal, dismissal or disqualification in the Best in Field competition will not affect a hound's prior awards earned on that day, but will count towards barring the hound from competition.

Section 10. At the option of the Host Club non-regular stakes may be offered as follows (all entries and awards shall be divided by breed):

Note: The following stakes are non-regular stakes which can be offered by the Host Club at its option. If one or more of these stakes is offered, it is simply noted and winners are determined from their performance in the regular stake. In other words, these are not stakes especially run. They are designed to offer competitors a chance to win special non-regular ribbons or prizes. No points are awarded in any of these stakes.

(a) Kennel Stake: For hounds of any individual breeds; an entry shall consist of two hounds designated at time of entry in one of the regular stakes being owned and kenneled by the same person.

(b) Veteran Stake: For any individual hound whose age exceeds six (6) years, except Irish Wolfhounds whose age shall exceed five (5) years.

(c) Breeder Stake: For any breed which shall have, designated at time of entry, two hounds bred by the same individual.

In all non-regular stakes there will be only one winner per breed with no championship points awarded.

Section 11. A person may handle any number of hounds during a trial, but may not handle more than one hound in each course of that trial.

Section 12. Any owner who deputizes another person to handle his hound must not interfere with the hound or handler throughout the duration of the course.

Section 13. Handlers shall use on each entry a simplified slip which will give almost instantaneous freedom to the hound which is to be released when the "Tally-Ho" signal is called by the Huntmaster. No metal leads or slips shall be permitted. Recommended slips are those consisting of a leather or webbing strap with a wide collar and double or single rings. No collar or paraphernalia shall be on the hound during the running of the course except the blanket (and muzzle where permitted or required); protective coverings in colors other than those listed in Section 5(h), are acceptable. No spike or prong collars are permitted on the field of a Lure Field Trial.

Section 14. These rules permit a handler to muzzle his hound, provided said muzzle has no sharp, hard edges, and allows the hound to breathe freely.

Section 15. A hound may not be added to a course, unless that hound is a regular entry and is to be scored (i.e., there shall be no bye-dog).

CHAPTER VI
Records & Fees Forwarded to ASFA

Section 1. All records must be received by the ASFA Records Coordinator within fourteen (14) days or be postmarked within ten (10) days of the approved Lure Field Trial. For penalty assessed for late receipt of records, see paragraph (h). These records must include:

(a) A copy of the approved Premium List.

(b) Names and complete addresses of all Judges and the Field Secretary.

(c) All completed entry forms.

(d) All Judge's(s') sheets, including re-runs and run-offs if required.

(e) All Record Sheets for every course, including re-runs and runoffs if required. The Host Club shall maintain a duplicate set of record sheets for its files.

(f) Notations of reasons why hounds who were entered did not run, e.g., absent, bitches in season, lame, dismissed, disqualified under the ASFA breed disqualifications, excused by the Field Chairman, etc.

(g) A per capita fee, as set by the Board of Directors (see schedule of fees in current issue of *Field Advisory News*) for each hound which was a paid entry (excepting those whose entry fee was refunded) in a regular stake shall be received by the ASFA Records Coordinator within fourteen (14) days or be postmarked within ten (10) days of the Lure Field Trial. Points are not recorded by the Records Coordinator until this per capita fee is received. The per capita must be paid by certified check, money order or club check (do not send cash or personal checks).

(h) The penalty charge for late receipt or postmark of records shall not exceed the per capita fee, subject to review by the ASFA Board of Directors.

(i) Changes to the approved Premium List will be accompanied by a letter of explanation to the Records Coordinator.

Section 2. The Records Coordinator will correct Field Clerk errors and placements on record sheets, where appropriate, but will not change any Judge's total score. The Records Coordinator will notify the Field Secretary of the Host Club of any and all such changes.

CHAPTER VII

Placements, Awards and Titles

Section 1. Placements

Championship points are not official until published in the *Field Advisory News*. In the event of an error in scoring, the Records Coordinator will notify the Host Club which shall have the sole responsibility of notifying those individuals whose hounds have received placements. Championship points in all regular stakes—open and field champion— shall be awarded by the ASFA on the basis of:

> *First Place*: Four times the number of hounds competing in the stake with a maximum of 40 points.
>
> *Second Place*: Three times the number of hounds competing in the stake with a maximum of 30 points.
>
> *Third Place*: Two times the number of hounds competing in the stake with a maximum of 20 points.
>
> *Fourth Place*: Points equal to the number of hounds competing in the stake with a maximum of 10 points.
>
> *NBQ (Next Best Qualified)*: No points awarded.

No hound shall receive a placement or be awarded points if it does not score at least 50 percent of the total possible combined scores. Hounds which do not receive placements under this provision will nevertheless be considered as in competition for the purpose of awarding points to hounds which do place.

Section 2. Awards

All host clubs shall use the following colors for their prize ribbons or rosettes:

First Place .... Blue

Second Place .... Red

Third Place	Yellow
Fourth Place	White
NBQ	Green
Best of Breed	Purple and Gold
Best in Field	Red, White, Blue

Each ribbon shall bear at least the following information: (a) club name or initials, (b) ASFA or American Sighthound Field Association spelled out, and (c) placement. Ideally, the ribbons or rosettes should be at least two (2) inches wide and approximately eight (8) inches long.

If ribbons or rosettes are awarded at fun or practice events they shall only be the following colors, but may be of any design or size:

First Place	Rose
Second Place	Brown
Third Place	Light Green
Fourth Place	Gray
NBQ	Light Pink
Best of Breed	Orange
Best in Field	Lavender

Section 3. Titles

Field Champion: A permanent title of Field Champion (F. Ch.) shall be awarded as a suffix to the registered name of any hound which has fulfilled the following championship requirements:

(a) Attained a number of championship points in Open Stake competition, as fixed by the ASFA. That number of points is 100.

(b) Contained in this 100 points there must be two (2) first placements or one (1) first placement and two (2) second placements.*All such placements shall be with competition which shall mean defeating at least one placing hound. In other words, a hound may have more than the 100 points but not be awarded the Field Champion title until the placements have been attained.

(c) Individuals wishing to know their hound's point standing should send the hound's registered name, registration number and a self-addressed stamped envelope to the Records Coordinator of the ASFA, and this information will be sent to them.

---

*Prior to June 1, 1982, a field championship will also be awarded if three second placements are included in the 100 points.

124

Lure Courser of Merit: The ASFA shall recognize and make appropriate awards to those hounds who have attained the Field Championship, and who after receiving the championship continue to compete and receive four (4) first placements with competition and 300 more points, which must be in the Field Champion stake. Hounds who shall have attained said number of placements and points shall be known as Lure Courser of Merit (LCM).

When a hound completes the LCM title it may continue to compete for additional titles. After receiving an additional four (4) first placements with competition and an additional 300 points, the title of LCM II shall be awarded. This process will be indefinitely repeatable for LCM III, IV, and so on.

The accumulation of placements and points for this title shall be retroactive.

CHAPTER VIII
Disqualification and Reinstatement of Hounds

Section 1. A hound's privilege to compete will be withdrawn upon either a disqualification or two (2) dismissals within six (6) Lure Field Trials. The Records Chairman of the ASFA must inform, in writing, the individual or individuals whose hound was disqualified, and cite the reason given for the hound's disqualification. (See Chapter III, Sections 12 and 13.)

Section 2. The privilege to compete may be reinstated by the Board of Directors upon completion of:

(a) a minimum of a calendar month of retraining as appropriate, and

(b) certification in writing by two (2) Regularly Licensed Judges for the breed being reinstated, stating the hound is running cleanly with two (2) other hounds of the same breed, and

(c) a letter to the Board of Directors from the owner of the hound applying for reinstatement, and

(d) a decision by the Board to reinstate said privilege.

CHAPTER IX
Protesting the Lure Field Trial

Any member of a club sanctioned to hold a Lure Field Trial, or any participant in the Lure Field Trial, or any individual belonging to a club sanctioned by the ASFA may lodge a "protest of proceedings" should he/she desire to do so. The following procedure must be followed:

Section 1. A written statement lodging the protest and explicitly describing the infringement or non-regular procedure or ruling, accompanied by a ten dollar ($10.00) protest filing fee (when paying by check, the check should be made out to ASFA) is given to the Field Chairman during the trial hours. The Field Committee must make a ruling in writing as soon as possible during trial hours on that day, a copy of which shall be given, on that day, to the protestor. All monies, copies of the protest and copies of the Field Committee rulings must be received by the ASFA Corresponding Secretary within fourteen (14) days of the trial or be postmarked within ten (10) days of the trial, except protests upheld by the Field Committee are cause for reimbursement of the $10 fee to the protestor and no monies shall be forwarded to the Corresponding Secretary.

Section 2. If an appeal of the decision of the Field Committee is desired, an additional letter from the protestor must be received by the ASFA Corresponding Secretary within fourteen (14) days or be postmarked within ten (10) days of the trial.

Section 3. The Corresponding Secretary will convey the protest situation to the Board of Directors of the ASFA, which shall rule on upholding or negating the protest.

Section 4. Protests upheld may void all points awarded at a Lure Field Trial or may result in other action deemed appropriate by the Board of Directors.

    (a) Protests upheld are cause for reimbursement of the $10.00 filing fee to the protesting individual.

    (b) Protests not upheld cause forfeit of the $10.00 filing fee to the Treasury of the ASFA.

Section 5. In all cases, the individual protesting is informed of the ruling on the protest appeal within 30 days subsequent to the ensuing Board of Directors meeting.

Section 6. When a protest voids points awarded, the Corresponding Secretary informs the Records Coordinator and he/she notifies all participants who had received points that they are voided for that Lure Field Trial.

Section 7. Statements of irregularity shall be sent to the ASFA Corresponding Secretary within 30 days after publication (in *Field Advisory News*) of the trial results in question.

CHAPTER X

Breed Disqualifications

The ASFA will accept and abide by all AKC breed standards and disqualifications for the ASFA-recognized sighthound breeds.

Pharaoh Hounds: Any solid white spot on the back of neck, shoulder, or any part of the back or sides of the dog.

Scottish Deerhounds: White blaze on the head, or a white collar.

Whippets: Blue or wall eyes; undershot/overshot one-quarter inch or more; coat other than short, close, smooth and firm in texture. Size: dogs 19 to 22 inches; bitches 18 to 21 inches; both to be measured across the shoulders at the highest point; one-half inch above or below the stated measurements will disqualify.

NOTE: There are no disqualifications for the other sighthound breeds.

CHAPTER XI

Licensing of Judges

Only those persons whose names appear on the List of Eligible Judges of the ASFA, which will be published from time to time in the *Field Advisory News*, may, in the discretion of the ASFA, be approved to judge at any ASFA sanctioned Lure Field Trial.

Section 1. General Requirements

All of the following requirements must be met before a license is granted:

(a) must be 18 years of age or older
(b) must be in good standing with the American Sighthound Field Association
(c) must certify that he regularly receives a copy of the *Field Advisory News*
(d) must have a general knowledge of the coursing abilities of purebred sighthound breeds recognized by the ASFA
(e) must be familiar with the *ASFA's Running Rules and Field Procedures—Lure Field Trials*

(f) must have participated in Lure Field Trials in some official capacity

(g) must have had lure coursing or open field coursing experience

(h) must file appropriate application forms

(i) must pay applicable fees.

Section 2. For the provisions of this Chapter only, the following terms shall be defined as follows:

Applicant: a person seeking change from previous status.

Apprentice: a person seeking a Provisional license to judge; has no status as a Judge at trials at this time.

Chairman: the ASFA Chairman of the Subcommittee on Judges' Licensing.

Judge (also, Regular Licensed, Licensed Judge): a person who is fully licensed for a breed with no restrictions. At any time the word "Provisional" or "Apprentice" does not precede the word "Judge," it shall mean an individual who is licensed without restriction for that breed.

Provisional (also, Provisionally Licensed, Provisional Judge): a person who may judge sanctioned Lure Field Trials, with restrictions, as noted in this chapter.

Publication: an applicant's name shall be published in *Field Advisory News* or any other method of publication as approved by the Board of Directors.

Trial: an ASFA-sanctioned Lure Field Trial at which ASFA points are awarded to appropriate hounds (i.e., not a Fun Trial).

Section 3. Pre-Licensing Requirements (Apprentice Status)

(a) Any person who seeks a Provisional License to judge must, in addition to fulfilling all of the general requirements of Section 1, apprentice judge a breed:

1. at a minimum of three trials, and
2. under three different Licensed Judges.

The applicant shall judge at least an entire breed, scoring each and every hound running in every course of that breed. Each of five breeds must be judged this minimum number of times before an apprentice is eligible for a Provisional License.

(b) The Apprentice Judge's sheets shall be accumulated until the requirements have been completed, including having each Licensed Judge fill out and sign an Apprentice Judging Confirmation Statement as approved by the ASFA. (See sample form in Appendix [page 141].)

(c) When the above requirements have been met, the sheets, together with the completed application form, shall be sent to the Chairman of Licensing. Upon receipt of this information, the Chairman shall verify the application, and may grant the Provisional License after two publications.

Section 4. Provisional Status (seeking Regular License)

(a) During the period for which a Provisional License is granted, the applicant is free to accept judging assignments. (On all Premium Lists, announcements, flyers, and so forth, an asterisk preceding the Judge's name shall denote Provisional.) The Provisional License encompasses all breeds, but at no time shall a person judge more than three breeds for which he is not regularly licensed at any one trial without special dispensation as stated in Section 8 of this chapter.

(b) Any person seeking a Regular License for a breed must judge the performance of seven or more hounds per trial in that breed:

1. at a minimum of three trials, and
2. under three or more different Licensed Judges.

The Provisional Judge shall on each occasion present the Licensed Judge with a form (see sample) as approved by the ASFA, which the Licensed Judge completes, signs, and returns to the Provisional Judge for mailing to the Chairman.

(c) When the above requirements have been met, the Provisional Judge shall notify the Chairman in writing, listing each breed and assignment, accompanied by the forms signed by each Licensed Judge for each judging assignment.

(d) The Board, upon recommendation of the Chairman, and after publication, shall determine if the applicant shall be granted a license for the breed or breeds for which the license is sought.

Section 5. Licensing for Additional Breeds. Any Judge regularly licensed in at least three breeds may seek an additional breed by meeting the following requirements:

(a) Judge provisionally the breed for which the license is sought at no less than three trials with three different Licensed Judges. (Judging seven hounds per breed is a requirement for the first three breeds only and does not apply to any breeds thereafter.)

(b) When the requirements of Section 5(a) have been met, notify the Chairman, in writing, that a license for one or more breeds is being sought, listing breed and assignment.

(c) The Board, upon recommendation of the Chairman and after the applicant's name has been published, shall determine whether the applicant shall be granted a license to judge the breed(s) for which the license is sought.

Section 6. No person shall accept a fee for judging, but may accept reimbursement from the Host Club to defray expenses.

Section 7. (a) Application and/or renewal fees, if any, for a license shall be set by the Board. Renewals, if any, shall be payable on or before the 1st of May of each year. This fee may, at the discretion of the Board, be changed from time to time; under no circumstances shall it be refundable.

(b) If the ASFA records indicate that a person has not judged at a trial in the preceding two years, the license shall lapse and the Judge shall lose all previous status.

Section 8. In each case where a Provisional or Licensed Judge is to judge more than three breeds provisionally at one trial, the respective Regional Director must write a letter of approval to the Scheduling Chairman in advance of, or together with, the sample Premium List. There will be no exception without such written dispensation.

Section 9. Two Provisional Judges may be scheduled to judge a breed; however, the assignment shall not count toward fulfilling the licensing requirements of either Judge.

Section 10. Upon receipt of written request from a Judge licensed for eight breeds, the Chairman may grant a license for all breeds.

Section 11. The Board of Directors may, after due and proper consideration, and after hearing all arguments presented, revoke or suspend a Judge's License for cause in which his performance, or lack of performance, has substantially compromised his effectiveness as a Judge. Reports of alleged misconduct should be sent to the ASFA Corresponding Secretary.

CHAPTER XII
Field Representatives

The Board of Directors shall be empowered to appoint, from time to time, Field Representatives who shall be charged with certain responsibilities and obligations, and who shall report directly to the Board or its designated committee.

CHAPTER XIII

Lure Field Trial Glossary of Terms

AKC: American Kennel Club.

ASFA: American Sighthound Field Association.

Blanket: A colorful cloth, without visible ornamentation, worn by the hounds during a course. The colors are bright yellow, bright pink and bright blue.

Course: Consists of 1, 2 or 3 hounds pursuing a lure of either mechanical or electrical drive over a selected course pattern. The course begins after the handlers' affirmative response to "Are you ready?" and ends when all hounds in the course are under handlers' physical restraint.

Course delay: A course delay shall include delays caused by hounds whose handlers delay the start of the course, hounds that break away from and avoid their handlers prior to the request "Are you ready?" and hounds that avoid their handlers after the command "retrieve your hounds."

Decision: Any official disposition of a hound by a Judge other than a score: e.g., an excusal, dismissal or disqualification.

Draw: A random drawing determining the order in which the hounds will run.

Handle: To take a hound to a Lure Field Trial as the owner's representative.

Host Club: The sanctioned club responsible for conducting the Lure Field Trial.

No-Course: Any course that a Judge determines to be unjudgable.

Pre-slip: Where a hound is slipped before the signal is given by the Huntmaster.

Qualifying score: 50 percent of the total possible combined scores from the preliminary and final courses.

Runoff: A competition to determine a final placement.

Score: A numerical figure given by a Judge to a hound in competition.

Stake: Composed of a number of courses where hounds compete against one another for championship points.

Trial Hours: Shall begin at the time stated in the Premium List for that trial and shall conclude one hour after the last scored course of the day.

NOTE: For the purpose of these regulations, words used in the masculine gender include the feminine and the feminine the masculine, and the singular the plural and the plural the singular.

APPENDIX

General Information on ASFA Policies and Procedures

The following information is provided here for convenient access. It is not a part of the *ASFA Running Rules and Field Procedures*. Please see the most recent issue of *Field Advisory News* for the names and addresses of the current ASFA Officials.

■ *Field Advisory News*

FAN is the official publication of, and is distributed by, the American Sighthound Field Association. *FAN* is the complete source of current information on the sport of lure coursing, regularly including:

- Lure Field Trial results
- official ASFA news
- list of upcoming trials
- list of ASFA member and affiliated clubs
- schedule of fees
- where to write
- list of available ASFA publications
- new Field Champions and Lure Coursers of Merit.

For more information contact:

Vicky Clarke, Editor
Field Advisory News
P.O. Box 399
Alpaugh, CA 93201

■ Applying for ASFA Affiliation

In order for a club to be granted Affiliate status with the ASFA and hold sanctioned Lure Field Trials, it is necessary for the club to meet the following requirements in the following order:

a. Make proper application to the ASFA Membership Chairman.

132

Applications must be accompanied by payment of dues, a list of members and officers of the club, with addresses, and an acceptable club Constitution.

b. Obtain approved dates for the holding of two Fun Lure Field Trials from the Scheduling Committee, following all current rules and procedures.

c. Hold at least two Fun Trials, following all ASFA Running Rules except as noted in (f). All entry forms, Judges' sheets, record sheets, and a copy of the Premium List for each trial must be forwarded to the Records Coordinator in accordance with Chapter VI.

d. Be in existence for one year or more.

e. Be approved by the ASFA as an Affiliated club.

f. The following rules apply to Fun Lure Trials ONLY:
1. No per capita fee is submitted with the fun trial results.
2. Judges need not be recognized nor licensed by the ASFA, but there must be two judges for each breed.
3. "NO ASFA POINTS SHALL BE AWARDED AT THIS FUN TRIAL" shall be printed on the front cover of the Fun Trial Premium List and entry form.
4. A Novice Stake is permitted. (See Novice Stake Guidelines.)
5. Ribbon colors. (See Ch. VII, Sec. 2.)
6. A copy of the approved Premium List must be sent to the Membership Committee Chairperson and to the appropriate Regional Director.

■ Applying for ASFA Membership

In order for a club to be granted Membership status with the ASFA and have a vote on all matters before the membership, it is necessary for the club to meet the following requirements:

a. Make proper application to the ASFA Corresponding Secretary. The application must be accompanied by a current list of members and officers of the club, including addresses, and a current constitution. Dues must be current with the ASFA.

b. The club must have held two separate Lure Field Trials on two separate weekends in each of the previous two years. The results of these trials must have been published in *FAN*.

The application for Membership will be presented to the ASFA Board of Directors, together with the Membership Committee recommendation, for a decision within 90 days after completed filing.

■ Novice Stake Guidelines

1. Hounds will run the course alone.
2. Order of running will be determined by random law and entered onto the Record Sheet (and Draw Order, if used) as 1-Y, 1-P, 1-B, 2-Y, etc.
3. Judges will score each hound using one Judge's Sheet for three Novice hounds.
4. Scores shall be posted on the Record Sheet in the usual manner.
5. Placements will be awarded based on the combined Preliminary and Final scores.
6. The winner of this stake will not be eligible to compete in the Best of Breed course with the winners of the Open and Field Champion Stakes.
7. Novice Stake records shall be forwarded to the Records Coordinator with the other stakes and shall count in the total number of hounds entered in a Fun Trial for evaluation of the Club's ability to handle paperwork. Novice Stake paperwork must be clearly labeled as such.
8. The entry fee for any stake at a fun trial shall be left to the discretion of the Host Club. Fees may vary to encourage entries in a stake.
9. It is strongly recommended that each club holding Fun Trials offer a Novice Stake and encourage owners of hounds that have not been properly trained to enter this stake.
10. If a Novice Stake is offered, it will appear in the club's Premium List.

■ Singles Stake Guidelines

1. See Novice Guidelines number 1 through 6.
2. Singles Stake records shall be forwarded to the Records Corodinator appropriately labeled as such. The per capita fee is due for each hound run.
3. The entry fee shall be the same as the regular stakes.
4. ASFA shall publish first through NBQ of each Singles Stakes.
5. When entries warrant a Singles Breed Stake, the Judge(s) shall be the same as the regular stakes of that breed and the stake should be run in conjunction with the other stakes of that breed. In a Mixed Singles Stake, the club shall choose one or two from those Judges listed for the trial and announce the Judge(s) and order of running to the entrants.

6. Hounds with breed disqualifications and/or hounds that have been disqualified from competition in other stakes are eligible to enter the Singles Stake.
7. When a Singles Stake is offered, owners of hounds that have not been properly trained should be encouraged to enter this stake.

■ Invitationals

Each year the ASFA will sanction a series of Lure Field Trials, the purpose of which shall be to promote and further test those hounds that have attained a certain number of points toward their Field Championship, and those hounds that are Field Champions or Lure Coursers of Merit of record.

The Regional Invitational

Each year the ASFA will sanction a series of Lure Field Trials, the purpose of which shall be to promote and further test those hounds that have attained a certain number of points toward their Field Championship and hounds that have earned the Field Champion or Lure Courser of Merit titles.

Requesting permission. The club submits a request to its Regional Director at least 4 months prior to the proposed date. This request should include:

- Name of the club
- Proposed date
- Location of trial and description of the grounds
- Entry fee
- Additional activities (if any)

Date. Regional Invitationals must be held between June 1st and December 31st. A date that has already been approved by the Scheduling Chairman for a trial in that region cannot be used. After a date has been approved for the Regional Invitational no other trial shall be held in the region on the same date.

Location and grounds. The trial must be held within regional boundaries. The grounds must be adequate to accommodate a large trial for the region. Course lengths must be within rule specifications (500 yards or more), but a length in excess of 750 yards is recommended. The grass must be a length that allows the Lure Operator clear visibility of the lure. Consideration should also be given to accessibility, lodging, refreshments and rest room facilities.

Entry fees. Minimum entry fee is $10.00 for pre-entries; if late entries are accepted, minimum is $15.00.

Additional activities. Activities such as banquets, seminars, dog shows, awards, etc. (if offered) should be listed.

Eligibility. Any hound that has earned at least one ASFA point, or equivalent point in its country of residence, or is a Field Champion of record, is eligible to enter. An eligible hound may be entered in any number of Regional Invitationals.

FAN *publication*. One full page will be available for each Regional Invitational provided the host club submits ad copy at least 90 days before the trial. Two full pages (including photos) will be made available after the trial. The article and photos, if any, should be submitted as soon as possible after the trial to insure timely publication. There is no charge to the host club for these publications.

Per capita fees to ASFA. A per capita fee of $4.00 per hound will be forwarded to the Records Coordinator with the trial results.

Rosettes and trophies. ASFA provides rosettes for all placements and ASFA medallions for each Best of Breed winner; the host club must request these at least 60 days before the trial. The host club may offer additional trophies at their own expense or through donations.

General. The Premium List shall include both Host Club and ASFA Officers and Board Members. Judges should be regularly licensed for the breeds that they judge. Equipment provided by the Host Club should be adequate to handle a large entry for the region. A veterinarian should be on call or at the trial site.

Each year, the Regional Director will review all proposals received from clubs requesting to host a Regional Invitational. After a decision has been made, the Regional Director shall notify each club that submitted a proposal of the decision.

All additional requirements and exceptions to the ASFA rulebook relating to Regional Invitationals are noted; all ASFA rules shall apply to Regional Invitationals. Exceptions to any of the above policies must be approved by the ASFA Board of Directors.

Consult the ASFA Corresponding Secretary or your Regional Director for more information.

■ Dual Champions and Dual Titlists

The ASFA shall recognize and make appropriate awards to those hounds who have attained the Field Championship and an AKC Show championship certificate. Recipients of said awards shall be known as Dual Champions.

The ASFA shall also recognize and make appropriate awards to those hounds that have obtained the Field Championship and any of the following awards:

1. AKC obedience or tracking title
2. AWC Award of Racing Merit certificate
3. NOTRA Oval Racing Champion certificate
4. NOFCA Coursing Champion or Courser of Merit award

Recipients of these awards shall be known as Dual Titlists.

■ Sample Forms and Premium List

Following are reduced copies of the standard ASFA Judges Sheet and Record Sheet, a sample Entry Form, and a sample Premium List. Single copies of these forms, as well as Protest Forms and other useful items, are available from the Corresponding Secretary.

Records Coordinator

■ Submission of Trial Results

Current points and placements of individual hounds can be determined by requesting this information in writing from the Records Coordinator. Include a stamped, self-addressed envelope with each request. A Field Secretary may accept entries of hounds that are pending individual registration. The Records Coordinator will record points and placements earned by such hounds for a limited period of time. For more information, contact the Records Coordinator or ASFA Corresponding Secretary.

■ Organization of Trial Records for Submission

The following required items must be promptly sent to the Records Coordinator following each trial, as indicated in Chapter VI:

1. Proper per capita check (current fee for each hound entered which has not been excused as lame or in season at or prior to Roll Call).
2. One copy of the approved Premium List, with corrections to list of Judges, if appropriate.
3. All Entry Forms, Judges' Sheets and Record Sheets, completely filled out and written legibly.

The preferred order to use in organizing this material for submission is:

[continued on page 142]

AMERICAN SIGHTHOUND FIELD ASSOCIATION
OFFICIAL JUDGE'S FORM

Host Club _____

Date _____

BREED (circle)	A Ba B G Ib IW P S SD W
STAKE (circle)	OPEN A B F.Ch. A B BOB BIF Runoff for _____ placement ☐
COURSE (circle)	Prelim Final 1 2 3 4 5 6 7 8 Course rerun ☐

JUDGE #1 _____

#2 _____
(Judge's signature)

(circle)

	yellow	pink	blue
Enthusiasm (15)			
Follow (15)			
Speed (25)			
Agility (25)			
Endurance (20)			
Preslip Penalty (−1 to −10)			
Course Delay Penalty (−1 to −10)			
TOTAL SCORE or excused, dismissed, disqualified			

	yellow	pink	blue
Reasons for excusal, dismissal or disqualification MUST BE FILLED OUT HERE			

Check for errors or omissions. Judge must initial changes or corrections. ASFA-0-7-9/80

Sample ASFA judge's form.

AMERICAN SIGHTHOUND FIELD ASSOCIATION - RECORD SHEET

		Hound Information		Preliminary				Final				Results				ASFA
Seq. #	Call Name	Registered Name	Registration Number	Course & Blanket	Judge 1 Score	Judge 2 Score	Total Score	Course & Blanket	Judge 1 Score	Judge 2 Score	Total Score	Combined Score	*Run-off	* BOB run	Place-ment	ASFA use only

BREED (circle)	STAKE (circle)	Host Club:	Judge # 1	
A Ba B	Open			
G Ib IW	A B C F.CH.	Date:		Field Clerk (Signature)
P S SD	BIF Single		Judge # 2	
W Prov.	Novice			Field Trial Secretary (Signature)

* Blanket color and total score only

ASFA-RS 4/91

Sample ASFA record sheet.

138

BORZOI CLUB OF AMERICA

Sunday, May 10, 1991   Entry Fee: $10.00 per hound

Entries close Tuesday, May 5, or when the limit of 75 hounds is reached.

Make checks payable to BCOA. Mail entries to:

Kathy Budney, 1098 New Britain Rd., Rocky Hill, CT 06067

I enclose $ _____ for entry fees   Conditional, unsigned, incomplete or unpaid entries will not be accepted.

Breed	Call Name	Sequence # to be assigned by Field Secretary
Registered Name of Hound		

Stake ☐ Open ☐ F Ch. ☐ Single   Additional Stakes ☐ Kennel ☐ Breeder ☐ Veteran

(Circle One)	Registration Number	Date of Birth
AKC Reg:		
AKC ILP:		Sex: ☐ Dog ☐ Bitch
NGA Volume & Certificate:		
Foreign # & Country:		Breeder (optional)
Name of actual owner(s)		Phone (optional)
Address		

City	State	Zip

Is this the first ASFA point trial for this hound? ☐ Yes (If yes, a new record must be established.)

Has any information changed since last ASFA trial entry? ☐ Yes

☐ If possible, please separate my hounds

I CERTIFY that I am the actual owner of this dog, or that I am the duly authorized agent of the actual owner whose name I have entered above. In consideration of the acceptance of this entry and of the opportunity to have this dog judged and to win prize money, ribbons, or trophies, I (we) agree to abide by the rules and regulations of the American Sighthound Field Association in effect at the time of this lure field trial and by any additional rules and regulations appearing in the premium list for this lure field trial. I (we) agree that the club holding this lure field trial has the right to refuse this entry for cause which the club shall deem to be sufficient. I (we) agree to hold this club, its members, directors, governors, officers, agents or other functionaries, any employees of the aforementioned parties and the owner(s) of the trial premises or grounds harmless from any claim for loss or injury which may be alleged to have been caused directly or indirectly to any person or thing by the act of this dog while in or upon the lure field trial premises or grounds or near any entrance thereto, and I (we) personally assume all responsibility and liability for any such claim, and I (we) further agree to hold the aforementioned parties harmless from any claim for loss of this dog by disappearance, theft, death or otherwise, and from any claim for damage or injury to the dog, whether such loss, disappearance, theft, damage or injury be caused or alleged to be caused by the negligence of the club, or any of the aforementioned parties, or by the negligence of any other person or any other cause or causes. I (we) certify and represent that the dog entered is not a hazard to persons or other dogs. This entry is submitted for acceptance of the foregoing representations and agreements.

SIGNATURE of owner or his agent

duly authorized to make this entry _____

ASFA 0-5-1/90

Sample ASFA entry form.

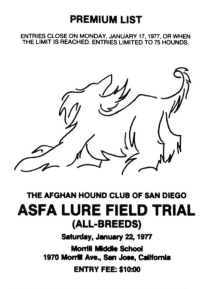

Sample premium list (outside front cover).

Sample premium list (inside front cover).

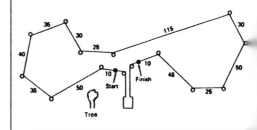

Sample premium list (inside back cover).

Camille Mendicino, Field Secretary
197 E. Nicodemus Road
Westminster, MD 21157

FIRST CLASS

Leigh Littleton
Rt. 2, Box 548
Fincastle, VA 24090

Sample premium list (outside back cover).

AMERICAN SIGHTHOUND FIELD ASSOCIATION

( ) APPRENTICE
( ) PROVISIONAL   JUDGING CONFIRMATION STATEMENT

I hereby certify that _____ ( ) apprentice   judged with
                name - please print   ( ) provisionally

me at the _____ lure field trial held on _____.
            club   date

The applicant judged all courses of all stakes (including run-offs and BOB runs) of
the following breeds:

Breed	Number Competing		Breed	Number Competing	
__ A	__ Open	__ F.Ch.	__ IW	__ Open	__ F.Ch.
__ Ba	__ Open	__ F.Ch.	__ P	__ Open	__ F.Ch.
__ B	__ Open	__ F.Ch.	__ S	__ Open	__ F.Ch.
__ G	__ Open	__ F.Ch.	__ SD	__ Open	__ F.Ch.
__ Ib	__ Open	__ F.Ch.	__ W	__ Open	__ F.Ch.

Based on my experience with this individual, I feel that he or she:
                       ( ) is well-qualified to be granted the license sought.
                       ( ) needs more experience before being granted a license.
                       ( ) other - please enter comments on the reverse side.

Name of Licensed Judge (please print): _____

Signature: _____   Date: _____

ASFA-O-17-7/83

Sample ASFA apprentice judge's form.

1. Per capita check
2. Premium List
3. Field Records in the following order:
   A. Afghan Hound
      1. Open Stake
         a. Entry Forms in sequence number order
         b. Record Sheets
         c. Preliminary course Judges' Sheets in course-number order.
         d. Final course Judges' Sheets in course-number order.
         e. Judges' Sheets from runoffs, if any.
      2. Field Champion Stake
         (a) through (e), as above
      3. Best of Breed run Judges' Sheets, if any. (Total scores and blanket colors are posted to the proper Record Sheet in column labeled "BOB Run.")
   B. Basenji (follow same order as above).
   C. Borzoi (follow same order as above), etc., by breed in alphabetical order.
   D. Best in Field Record Sheet (filled out completely).
   E. Best in Field Judges' Sheets in course-number order.

Copies of the Record Sheets must be retained for the club files. It is strongly recommended that copies of all forms, including entries, the Premium List, Judges' Sheets, etc., be kept, as well as proof of the date of mailing. If the original package is lost in the mail, the trial results can be reconstructed.

The preferred system for assigning sequence numbers to hounds is:

1–99	Afghan Hound
100s	Basenji
200s	Borzoi
300s	Greyhound
400s	Ibizan Hound
500s	Irish Wolfhound
600s	Pharaoh Hound
700s	Saluki
800s	Scottish Deerhound
900s	Whippet
1–49	indicates an Afghan Hound Open entry

51–99   indicates an Afghan Hound Field Champion entry
101–149   indicates a Basenji Open entry
151–199   indicates a Basenji Field Champion entry, etc.

■ Filling in the Trial Record Sheets

The Record Sheets must be completely and legibly filled out. This includes the complete names of the Judges, the complete names and registration numbers of the hounds, etc. If an entered hound is not competing, the reason should be entered on the Record Sheet, as should the reason for any excusal, dismissal or disqualification. For tie runoffs, the blanket color and total score only should be entered in the "Runoff" column; similarly, for Best of Breed runs, enter only these items in the "BOB Run" column.

Following are two examples of filled-in Record Sheets. The first includes the Open and Field Champion stakes for a breed with a small entry; the second is for Best in Field competition.

■ Revising the Running Rules

The procedure for revising the *Running Rules and Field Procedures* of the American Sighthound Field Association is given here. This has been adopted as a Special Rule of Order of the ASFA. As such it can be amended only by a two-thirds majority vote of a Convention of Delegates, to which prior notice has been given of the proposed amendment. Its provisions can, however, be suspended during a Convention of Delegates by approval of a motion to suspend the rules, requiring a two-thirds majority vote. (For discussion on the status of such a special rule, see the current edition of *Robert's Rules of Order, Newly Revised*.)

Section 1. Any member club may propose a rules change by submitting a detailed copy of the change to its Regional Director via its Club Delegate. (Such a proposed change is hereinafter called a proposal.)

Section 2. Sometime within each calendar year any Regional Director who has received rules change proposals in accordance with Section 1 above shall call a Regional Rules Conference to consider such proposals. A Regional Rules Conference may be conducted by mail.

Section 3. (a) A proposal which is passed by a Regional Rules Conference which has a majority of the clubs in the region represented is then

AMERICAN SIGHTHOUND FIELD ASSOCIATION - RECORD SHEET

Seq. #	Call Name	Registered Name	Registration Number	Prelim Course & Blanket	Prelim Judge 1 Score	Prelim Judge 2 Score	Prelim Total Score	Final Course & Blanket	Final Judge 1 Score	Final Judge 2 Score	Final Total Score	Combined Score	Run-off	BOB run	Placement	ASFA use only
301	Luke	Cool Hand Luke	HD 101233	1	Y	71	75	146	2 P	Exc	Dis.					Dis
302	Bullet	pending	pending	2	Y	71	75	146	2 Y	77	78	155	301	Y 155		BOB 1
303	Kari	Ch Anna Karenia COX	HM 103121-01	2	P	62	68	130	1 Y	85	86	171	301	P 153		2
304	Bugs	Im Bugs About Daddy	ILP 78410	1	B	Pulled by owner - Lame after Roll Call & Draw										
351	Slic	Ch Whos Slick As Ice CD Lcm	HD 201201	1	P	72	73	145	1 P	63	68	131	276	B 144		1
352	Minnie	Minnie Mouse Lcm V	Vol 87 20434	pulled In Season · refund											
S 301	Whee	Ch Whenever You Want CD	WY 201304	1	Y	50	49	99	1 Y	5	5	10	109			NQ
S 302	Janie	Janestown Jand	Vol 90 00011	absent											

BREED (circle): A Sa B / B Ib IW / P S SO / M Prov.
STAKE (circle): Open A B C / F.Ch. / BIF Single Novice
Host Club: Coastal Coursers
Dates: November 14, 1991
Judge #1: Larry Flynn
Judge #2: Dean Wright
Field Clerk (Signature): Lori Coulson
Field Trial Secretary (Signature): Camille Verdier
* Blanket color and total score only
ASFA-RS 4/91

AMERICAN SIGHTHOUND FIELD ASSOCIATION - RECORD SHEET

Seq. #	Call Name	Registered Name	Registration Number	Prelim Course & Blanket	Prelim Judge 1 Score	Prelim Judge 2 Score	Prelim Total Score	Final Course & Blanket	Final Judge 1 Score	Final Judge 2 Score	Final Total Score	Combined Score	Run-off	BOB run	Placement	ASFA use only
A 01	Tammi	Ch Tammie Till Us True	HD 782101	1	B	75		75								
BA 151	Blink	Blink And Her Gone CD	HM 304201-02	1	Y	pulled at line										
B 201	Soot	pending	pending	3	Y	75		75								
G 302	Bullet	pending	pending	2	B	76		76	2 Y	76		76				BIF
1B 451	Olea	Spanish Days & Nights	HD 721454	1	P	76		76	2 P	75		75				
P 651	Seker	Kamaraj Seker Lcm II	HD 028303	3	P	76		76	1 P	75		75				
S 701	Coco	Lazy Jones Brown Derby	HM 728324	2	Y	75		75								
V 951	Fact	Tennessee Fact Or Fiction Lcm VI	HD 221768	2	P	76		76	1 Y	74		74				

BREED (circle): A Sa B / C Ib IW / P S SO / W Prov.
STAKE (circle): Open A B C / F.Ch. / BIF Single Novice
Host Club: Coastal Coursers
Dates: November 14, 1991
Judge #1: Dean Wright
Judge #2: Camille Verdier
Field Clerk (Signature): Lori Coulson
Field Trial Secretary (Signature): Camille Verdier
* Blanket color and total score only
ASFA-RS 4/91

Sample ASFA record sheets, completed.

144

submitted by the Regional Director to the ASFA Rules Evaluation Committee. The Regional Director shall also submit the proposal to the *Field Advisory News* for publication with a notice that this proposal has been generated by the region and submitted to the Rules Evaluation Committee for consideration.

(b) Proposals submitted to the Rules Evaluation Committee and to *FAN* must be accompanied by appropriate explanatory material (i.e., "reason" for proposing the rule change and the "effect" of the rule change if passed).

(c) The Board of Directors may propose a rule change by submitting a detailed copy of the change to the Rules Evaluation Committee via the chairman of that committee.

Section 4. The Rules Evaluation Committee shall consist of three individuals appointed by the Board of Directors. The chairman of this committee shall be selected by the Board of Directors. The Rules Evaluation Committee may hold a meeting in conjunction with any Board of Directors meeting or may conduct meetings by mail whenever submitted proposals are outstanding.

Section 5. The Rules Evaluation Committee can discuss and/or amend a rule proposal. The committee shall edit all proposals for grammar and agreement with context of the ASFA rulebook. The committee shall investigate any possible contradictions with rules (other than the specific rule being considered for alteration) and shall report these contradictions (if any) with the final version of the proposal. The committee may suggest appropriate options to the proposal. The committee may generate proposals in response to issues raised by Regional Directors of the ASFA Board of Directors. The committee may not reject a properly submitted proposal, but shall have the obligation to recommend action on the proposal to the ASFA Convention of Delegates (see Sections 7 and 8).

Section 6. Proposals passed by the Rules Evaluation Committee as outlined previously shall be submitted to the *Field Advisory News* for publication with all appropriate explanatory material. Such proposals shall be published with a statement that this final version of the proposal will be submitted to the next Annual Convention of Delegates for a vote.

Section 7. Proposals passed by the Rules Evaluation Committee and published in the *Field Advisory News* as outlined previously, shall be submitted to the next Annual Convention of Delegates for a vote. Such proposals shall be circulated, with a notice that these proposals will be on the Convention agenda, to registered convention delegates, at least 30 days prior to the Convention.

Section 8. Only rule change proposals that have followed this procedure will be discussed at the Annual Convention of Delegates. No changes, alterations, modifications or new proposals shall be recognized.

Section 9. A proposal that has received a favorable vote at the Annual Convention of Delegates shall be considered a change to the *Running Rules and Field Procedures—Lure Field Trials*. Such proposals shall be published in the *Field Advisory News* in the first available issue and shall go into effect January 1 following the ratification.

Section 10. Approval of a proposal by the Annual Convention of Delegates shall not necessarily imply that a new edition of the rulebook be published. The Board of Directors will determine when a new version of the rulebook is needed.

ASFA CONSTITUTION AND BY-LAWS

Name and Objectives

Section 1. The name of the Association shall be the American Sighthound Field Association (ASFA).

Section 2. The objectives of the Association shall be:

(a) to promote and further the advancement of purebred sighthounds and to do all possible to bring their natural qualities to perfection;

(b) to protect and advance the interests of the sighthound breeds and to encourage sportsmanlike competition at purebred dog activities;

(c) to institute a system of competitive Lure Field Trials for sighthounds which will attempt to test their historical abilities by providing as realistic as possible a simulation of coursing;

(d) to issue appropriate certificates of recognition to those hounds proving their worth by competing in Association sanctioned Lure Field Trials;

(e) to direct Association efforts towards obtaining American Kennel Club recognition of a system of Lure Field Trials for sighthounds.

Section 3. The Association shall not be conducted or operated for profit and no part of any profits or remainder or residue from revenues generated by the Association shall enure to the benefit of any member club or individual.

ARTICLE II
Membership

Section 1. Eligibility. There shall be one type of membership open to all clubs or groups who subscribe to the purposes of this Association, who have been in active existence for two (2) years or longer and who have held two (2) or more successful sanctioned Lure Field Trials during each of those years; however, no club or group which, either according to its objectives or in fact, is operated for the financial benefit of its members, shall be eligible for membership in the Association.

Section 2. Dues. Membership dues shall be payable on or before the first day of May of each year, and shall be accepted only when accompanied by a list of names and addresses of the current officers of the club, and of the club delegate. No member club may vote whose dues are not paid for the current year. During the month of March the Treasurer shall send each member club a statement of its dues for the ensuing year.

Section 3. Election to Membership. Each applicant shall apply on a form as approved by the Board of Directors and which shall provide that the applicant agrees to abide by this Constitution and By-laws. This application shall state the name of the applicant club, names and complete addresses of its Board of Directors and current members, period of active existence and sanctioned Lure Field Trials held. Accompanying the application the prospective member club shall submit a copy of its constitution and by-laws as well as any other information required by the Board of Directors of the Association.

All applications are to be filed with the Corresponding Secretary and each application shall be considered and voted upon by the Board of Directors within ninety (90) days from the date of a completed filing. The Board of Directors shall consider such applications within the context of the policies regarding membership eligibility established by the Board and the Annual Convention of Delegates, which are in effect at the time the application is received.

Applicants for membership which have been rejected by the Board of Directors may request that their application be considered at the next Annual Convention of Delegates. In such cases the application shall be considered and voted upon immediately following the initial seating of delegates. If the applicant club is elected by a simple majority vote to membership, the Convention shall then consider and seat any delegates of such club under its normal procedures.

Section 4. Termination of Membership. Club membership may be terminated:

(a) by resignation. Any member club in good standing may resign from the Association upon written notice to the Corresponding Secretary; but no member club may resign when in debt to the Association. Dues obligations are considered a debt to the Association and they become incurred on the first day of each fiscal year.

(b) by lapsing. Any membership will be considered as lapsed and automatically terminated if such member club's dues remain unpaid ninety (90) days after the first day of the fiscal year; however, the Board of Directors may grant an additional ninety (90) days of grace to such delinquent member clubs in meritorious cases. In no case may a member club be entitled to vote whose dues are unpaid.

(c) by inactivity. Any member club which fails to hold an ASFA-sanctioned Lure Field Trial during a period of five consecutive calendar years shall automatically revert to Affiliate status. National clubs, as defined by the ASFA, are exempt from this provision.

ARTICLE III
Affiliation

Section 1. Eligibility. There shall be an affiliation open to all clubs or groups who subscribe to the purposes of this Association and who are eligible to apply for a sanctioned Lure Field Trial under the provisions for the current *Running Rules and Field Procedures—Lure Field Trials*.

Section 2. Dues. Affiliation dues shall be payable on or before the first day of May each year, and shall be accepted only when accompanied by a list of names and addresses of the current officers of the club and the person designated to be the ASFA correspondent. During the month of March the Treasurer shall send each affiliated club a statement of its dues for the ensuing year.

Section 3. Election to Affiliation. Each applicant club for affiliation shall apply on a form as approved by the Board of Directors and which shall provide that the applicant agrees to abide by this Constitution and By-laws. This application shall state the name of the applicant club, names and complete addresses of its Board of Directors and current members, period of active existence and a statement as to its eligibility to apply for a sanctioned Lure Field Trial under the provision of the current *Running Rules and Field Procedures—Lure Field Trials.* Accompanying the application, the prospective affiliated club shall submit a copy of its constitution and by-laws and an application fee, and such additional information as may be required by the Board of Directors of the Association.

All applications are to be filed with the Corresponding Secretary or Membership Chairman, and each application shall be considered and acted upon by the Board of Directors within ninety (90) days from the date of a completed filing. The Board of Directors shall consider such applications within the context of policies regarding eligibility for affiliation established by the Board and the Annual Convention of Delegates, which are in effect at the time the application is received.

Section 4. Termination of Affiliation.

Club affiliation may be terminated:

(a) by resignation. Any affiliated club in good standing may resign from the Association upon written notice to the Corresponding Secretary; but no affiliated club may resign when in debt to the Association. Dues obligations are considered a debt to the Association and they become incurred on the first day of each fiscal year.

(b) by lapsing. An affiliation will be considered as lapsed and automatically terminated if such affiliated club's dues remain unpaid ninety (90) days after the first day of the fiscal year; however, the Board of Directors may grant an additional ninety (90) days of grace to such delinquent affiliated clubs in meritorious cases.

ARTICLE IV
Voting and
Annual Convention of Delegates

Section 1. Club Delegates. On or before May 1 of each year, each member club will appoint a Club Delegate who shall represent the member club during the ensuing year. Notice of such appointments are to be filed with the Corresponding Secretary and shall be made on a form as approved by the Board of Directors. Names and addresses of all Club Delegates shall be printed in the July issue of the *Field Advisory News*. A member club may change its Club Delegate at any time by submitting a revised notice of appointment. An individual may be Club Delegate for at most one club.

Section 2. Annual Convention of Delegates. There shall be an Annual Convention of Delegates held in April of each year. The exact location shall be selected by the Annual Convention of Delegates two (2) years in advance of the convention. The location shall rotate across the country so that each section of the country will host the convention once every three (3) years. Sections are

> *West:* Regions 1, 2 and 3;
> *Central:* Regions 4, 5 and 6;
> *East:* Regions 7 and 8.

The date shall be selected by the Board of Directors. The date and location shall stand unless overridden by a two-thirds vote of the delegates in attendance at the ensuing Annual Convention of Delegates. Each member club shall be entitled to be represented by two (2) Convention Delegates, who shall be identified by the club on an appropriate form.

Section 3. Special Convention of Club Delegates. There shall be a special Convention of Club Delegates called by the Corresponding Secretary upon receipt of a petition signed by the Club Delegates of one-third of the member clubs in good standing. The petition shall state the date (at least 45 days after the date of the petition), location and purpose of such a Special Convention of Club Delegates and no other Association business shall be transacted thereat. Written notice of such a Special Convention of Club Delegates shall be mailed by the Corresponding Secretary at least thirty (30) days prior to the date of the Special Convention of Club Delegates. The quorum for such a meeting shall be a majority of the member clubs.

Section 4. Submission of Matters to Club Delegates During the Fiscal Year by the Board of Directors. The Board of Directors shall have the authority to poll the Club Delegates. The response to any such poll is to be considered by the Board of Directors in arriving at a decision regarding such matters; but, the ultimate responsibility for the decision remains with the Board of Directors. All actions of the Board of Directors are subject to review by Annual or Special Conventions of Delegates.

Section 5. Board of Directors Meetings. Regular meetings of the Board of Directors shall be held at least twice each fiscal year at such time and place as may be designated by the Board of Directors. Written notice of each such meeting shall be mailed by the Corresponding Secretary at least thirty (30) days prior to the date of the meeting. The quorum for such a meeting shall be a majority of the Board of Directors.

The Board of Directors shall have the authority to conduct its affairs by mail. Questions to be voted upon submitted by the President or by one-third of the members of the Board shall be distributed to members of the Board by the Corresponding Secretary within three (3) days of receipt. Each member of the Board shall have fifteen (15) days from the date of mailing to send comments to the Corresponding Secretary. Such comments and a ballot shall be distributed to the Board members by the Corresponding Secretary within three (3) days from the expiration of the period for comment. Each member of the Board shall then have fifteen (15) days from the date of mailing to return a marked ballot to the Corresponding Secretary. The Secretary shall tally the ballots received during the fifteen (15) days and, if a majority of the members of the Board have responded, shall record the vote on the question and distribute the results to the members of the Board.

Section 6. Special Board of Directors Meetings. Special meetings of the Board of Directors may be called by the President, and shall be called by the Corresponding Secretary upon receipt of a written petition signed by at least one half of the members of the Board. The petition shall state the date (at least 45 days after the date of the petition), location and purpose of such special meeting and no other Association business shall be transacted thereat. Written notice of such a meeting shall be mailed by the Corresponding Secretary at least thirty (30) days prior to the date of the meeting. The quorum for such a meeting shall be a majority of the Board.

Section 7. Voting. Each member club whose dues are paid for the current fiscal year shall be entitled to one (1) vote for each Convention Delegate in attendance (to a maximum of two) at any Annual Convention of Delegates; and to one (1) vote by their Club Delegate at a Special

Convention of Club Delegates. Proxy voting will not be permitted at any Convention of Delegates and each Delegate may represent only one (1) member club.

Each Director and/or Officer shall be entitled to one (1) vote at any Board meeting at which he is present. Proxy voting will not be permitted at any Board meeting.

ARTICLE V

Directors and Officers

Section 1. Board of Directors. The Board of Directors shall be comprised of six (6) officers (President, First Vice President, Second Vice President, Recording Secretary, Corresponding Secretary, and Treasurer), eight (8) Regional Directors, and the Immediate Past President. The Immediate Past President will hold this position for a single, two-year term. The six (6) officers shall be elected for two-year terms at the Annual Convention of Delegates held during even numbered years and the eight (8) Regional Directors shall be elected for two-year terms by the Club Delegates of the member clubs in the respective areas during odd numbered years as provided in Article VI and shall serve until their successors are elected. General management of the Association's affairs, within the policies set forth by the Annual or Special Convention of Delegates shall be entrusted to the Board of Directors. The Board of Directors shall have no authority to alter provisions of the *Running Rules and Field Procedures—Lure Field Trials.*

Section 2. Officers. The Association's Officers shall serve in their respective capacities both with regard to the Association and its Convention of Delegates and the Board of Directors and its meetings.

(a) The President shall preside at all Conventions of Delegates and meetings of the Board, and shall have the duties and powers normally appurtenant to the office of President in addition to those particularly specified by this Constitution and By-laws.

(b) The First Vice President shall preside at all Conventions of Delegates and meetings of the Board in the absence of the President.

(c) The Second Vice President shall preside at all Conventions of Delegates and meetings of the Board in the absence of the President and the First Vice President.

(d) The Recording Secretary shall keep a record of all Conventions of Delegates and meetings of the Board and of all matters of which a record shall be ordered by the Board or Conventions of Delegates. He shall keep a roll of the member clubs and affiliate clubs of the Association with their addresses and carry out such other duties as are prescribed in this Constitution and By-Laws.

(e) The Corresponding Secretary shall have charge of all correspondence and such other duties as are prescribed in this Constitution and By-Laws.

(f) The Treasurer shall collect and receive all monies due or belonging to the Association. He shall deposit same in a bank designated by the Board, in the name of the Association. His books shall be at all times open to inspection of the Board of Directors and he shall report to them at every meeting the condition of the Association's finances and every significant item of receipt or payment not before reported; and at the Annual Convention of Delegates he shall render an account of all monies received or expended during the previous fiscal year. The Treasurer shall be bonded in such amount as the Board of Directors shall determine.

(g) The performance of the duties of any of the members of the Board of Directors as provided for in this Constitution and By-Laws is the overall responsibility of the Board of Directors and such duties may be delegated as required by an affirmative vote of two-thirds of the membership of the Board of Directors.

Section 3. Regional Directors. The eight (8) Regional Directors shall represent the various regions of the country as defined below:

Region 1. Alaska, Idaho, Montana, Oregon, Washington

Region 2. Arizona, California, Hawaii, Nevada

Region 3. Colorado, New Mexico, Utah, Wyoming

Region 4. Arkansas, Louisiana, Oklahoma, Texas

Region 5. Iowa, Kansas, Minnesota, Missouri, Nebraska, North Dakota, South Dakota

Region 6. Illinois, Indiana, Kentucky, Michigan, Ohio, Wisconsin

Region 7. Alabama, Florida, Georgia, Mississippi, North Carolina, South Carolina, Tennessee

Region 8. Connecticut, Delaware, Maine, Maryland, Massachusetts, New Hampshire, New Jersey, New York, Pennsylvania, Rhode Island, Vermont, Virginia, West Virginia

Section 4. Removal. Such Officers and Directors may, for violation or dereliction of duty, be removed by a two-thirds majority vote of the then actual membership of the Board, provided that notice of consideration of such removal has been given at least thirty (30) days prior to the meeting at which it is to be voted upon.

Section 5. Vacancies. Any vacancies occurring among the Officers during the year shall be filled until the next Annual Convention of Delegates by an affirmative vote of a majority of the then members of the Board, except that a vacancy in the office of President shall be automatically filled by the First Vice President and the resulting vacancy in the office of First Vice President shall be automatically filled by the Second Vice President. Any vacancies occurring among the Regional Directors shall be filled by a majority of the votes by the Club Delegates representing the respective region.

ARTICLE VI
The Association Year,
Annual Convention of Delegates, Elections

Section 1. Association Year. The Association's fiscal year shall begin on the first day of April and end on the last day of March.

The Association's official year shall begin immediately at the conclusion of the Annual Convention of Delegates and shall continue through the next Annual Convention of Delegates.

Section 2. Annual Convention of Delegates. The Annual Convention of Delegates shall be held in the month of April at which elections shall be held as provided in Article V by secret, written ballot. Officers elected shall take office immediately upon conclusion of the Annual Convention of Delegates and each retiring Officer shall turn over to his successor in office all properties and records relating to that office within thirty (30) days after the Annual Convention of Delegates.

Section 3. Elections. The nominated candidate receiving a majority of the votes cast for each position shall be declared elected. If no candidate receives a majority of the votes cast, the candidate receiving the fewest number of votes shall be eliminated and a recasting of votes shall be taken.

Section 4. Nominations.

(a) The Board of Directors shall appoint a Nominating Committee at the time of each Annual Convention of Delegates held in an odd-numbered year. The Committee shall include one (1) member of the

Board of Directors and two (2) representatives from member clubs. The Committee shall submit a list of nominees for officers to be published in the *Field Advisory News* at least 150 days prior to the next Annual Convention of Delegates. Each member club shall have forty-five (45) days following such publication to submit additional nominees for Officers which shall be circulated to each member club. Such nominations must be agreed to by the nominee and carry the endorsement of the nominating member club, written copies of both of which shall be submitted to the Corresponding Secretary.

(b) Candidates for office may also be nominated from the floor at the Annual Convention of Delegates. At the time of the election each candidate for office must be a Convention Delegate in attendance at such Annual Convention of Delegates.

(c) Nomination and election for each office shall be held in the order of the offices in Article V. Delegates may be nominated for more than one (1) office but may be elected to only one (1). No Delegate may be nominated for an office who has been elected to that office in each of the preceding two (2) terms; nor may any Delegate be nominated or accept a nomination who has, within the preceding year, accepted a fee, over and above expenses, for handling a hound at a sanctioned Lure Field Trial, or for performing or assisting in the performance of the duties of the officials of a sanctioned Lure Field Trial.

(d) Candidates for Regional Directors shall be nominated by the Club Delegates from member clubs located in each respective region during the month of October of each even-numbered year. Such nominations shall be sent to the Corresponding Secretary and shall be accompanied by written acceptance of the nominee. No person may be nominated or accept a nomination as Regional Director who has been elected to the position of Regional Director in each of the preceding two terms, or who has, within the preceding year, accepted a fee over and above expenses for handling a hound at a sanctioned Lure Field Trial, or for performing or assisting in the performance of the duties of the officials of a sanctioned Lure Field Trial. No Club Delegate may nominate more than one candidate for Regional Director. The Corresponding Secretary shall send each Club Delegate a ballot including such nominees by the 15th of the following November. Each Club Delegate shall then have until January 1 to return a marked ballot to the Corresponding Secretary. The Corresponding Secretary shall tally the ballots received by January 8 which were posted on or before January 1, and record the vote. The candidate receiving a majority of the votes cast in each region shall be declared elected. If no candidate receives a majority of the votes cast, only the two candidates (more only if required by a tie) receiving the highest number of votes will be included on the reballot. The Corresponding Secretary shall then notify all candidates, member and affiliated clubs in the respective region of the election results, including the elected candidate who shall take office immediately. At the time of elections, candidates for Regional Director must reside in the respective region. Only Club Delegates from member clubs in each region are eligible to vote for such Regional Director.

ARTICLE VII

Committees

Section 1. Appointments. The Board of Directors each year shall appoint standing committees to advance the work of the Association. Such committees shall be subject to the final authority of the Board. Special committees may also be appointed by the Board or by a Convention of Delegates to perform a particular function.

Section 2. Termination. Any committee appointment may be terminated by an affirmative vote of a majority of the membership of the Board (if appointed by the Board), or a majority of the Delegates in attendance at a Convention of Delegates, upon written notice to the appointee. Successors to those persons whose services have been terminated may be appointed.

Section 3. Standing Committees. Standing Committees shall include, but not be limited to the following:

1. Scheduling Committee
2. Membership Committee
3. Nominating Committee
4. Judging Committee
5. Rules Committee
6. Annual Convention of Delegates Committee
7. Field Trial Regulation Committee
8. Finance and Budget Committee

ARTICLE VIII

Discipline

Section 1. Any Member or Affiliate club or any individual who is suspended from the privileges of the American Kennel Club automati-

156

cally shall be suspended from the privileges of the ASFA for a like period.

Section 2. Any club or individual may prefer charges against any individual or club for alleged misconduct prejudicial to the best interests of the ASFA or any and all breeds of sighthounds. Written charges with specifications must be filed with the Corresponding Secretary together with a deposit of $25 which shall be forfeited if such charges are not sustained by the Board following a hearing. The Corresponding Secretary shall promptly distribute a copy of the charges to each member of the Board and the Board shall first consider whether it shall entertain jurisdiction in the matter. If the Board entertains jurisdiction of the charges, it shall fix a date of a hearing at the next regular Board meeting not less than six (6) weeks thereafter. The Corresponding Secretary shall promptly send one (1) copy of the charges to the accused by registered mail together with a notice of the hearing and an assurance that the defendant club or individual may personally appear in his own defense and bring witnesses if they (he/she) wish(es).

Section 3. Should the charges be sustained after hearing all the evidence and testimony presented by complainant and defendant, the Board may, by a two-thirds majority vote of those present, suspend the defendant from all privileges of the ASFA for a finite period of time following the date of the hearing. In such case the suspension shall not restrict the defendant's right to appear before the ensuing Annual Convention of Delegates. Immediately after the Board has reached a decision, its findings shall be put in written form and filed with the Recording Secretary. The Corresponding Secretary in turn shall notify each of the parties of the Board's decision and penalty, if any.

Section 4. The suspended club or individual shall have the right to appear before the next Annual Convention of Delegates to protest the terms of the suspension; and while no evidence shall be heard at the Convention, the Convention may, by a majority vote, modify the terms of the suspension and may specify conditions and a date for the ultimate reinstatement of the suspended party back into full privileges with the ASFA.

Section 5. (a) Host clubs that fail to meet and comply with the *Running Rules and Field Procedures—Lure Field Trials* are subject to suspension of any or all privileges, or to a fine, as may be deemed appropriate by the Board of Directors. Any fine imposed may be appealed to the Board of Directors.

157

(b) Individuals or clubs with outstanding debts to the ASFA are subject to suspension of any or all privileges by the Board of Directors.

(c) Before suspension of a club or individual is imposed, the Board shall offer the club or individual an opportunity to present any defense it may have.

(d) Under no circumstances does such suspension prohibit a club or individual from appearing before the Board and/or ensuing Annual Convention of Delegates and either body may rescind the suspension. Any suspension imposed in accordance with this section may be appealed to the next Annual Convention of Delegates according to the provisions of Section 4.

Section 6. Club privileges which may be suspended include, but are not limited to: eligibility to hold ASFA-sanctioned Lure Field Trials, voting, and being represented by a voting delegate at the Convention of Delegates. Individual privileges which may be suspended include, but are not limited to: acting as a member of the Board of Directors, representing a club as club delegate, and officiating or judging at a sanctioned Lure Field Trial. In addition, recording of points or placements that are earned by any hound owned by an individual may be suspended.

ARTICLE IX
Recognition of
Additional Sighthound Breeds

The procedure for recognizing an additional breed as eligible to enter ASFA-sanctioned Lure Field Trials is given herein, in chronological order.

Section 1. In order to be considered by ASFA for recognition, applicant organization must officially represent a sighthound breed which is a breed recognized by the AKC.

Section 2. Proposing an Additional Recognized Breed. Subsequent to receipt by the ASFA Corresponding Secretary of a request for recognition from a major national breed organization, that breed may be proposed for recognition either by:

(a) a two-thirds majority vote of the Annual Convention of Delegates, or

(b) petition of two-thirds of the ASFA member clubs.

158

Section 3. Evaluating a Proposal. After a proposal for recognizing an additional breed is made, as defined previously in Section 2, the Board of Directors shall investigate the potential advantages and disadvantages of such recognition. The Board of Directors shall report the results of the investigation to the first Annual Convention of Delegates falling at least six (6) months after the proposal is made.

Section 4. Approving Provisional Recognition. Upon completion of the steps given in Sections 2 and 3, the Annual Convention of Delegates may, by majority vote, approve provisional recognition of the breed. If the Convention approves provisional recognition of an additional breed, the breed shall be provisionally recognized until the following Annual Convention of Delegates; if provisional recognition is not approved, the proposal lapses.

Section 5. Provisional Recognition. During the provisional recognition period, the breed shall be eligible to be entered in ASFA-sanctioned Lure Field Trials, and trial results for the breed shall be recorded and published in the same manner as for any fully recognized breed. However, during this period, no ASFA title or certificate shall be awarded to any member of the breed.

Section 6. Full Recognition. The next Annual Convention of Delegates following provisional recognition shall vote on whether to accord the breed full recognition. Approval of full recognition shall require a two-thirds majority vote of the Delegates present. When a breed is fully recognized, it shall assume the same status as any previously recognized breed, and any appropriate titles and certificates, or points toward such titles and certificates, shall then be awarded to the members of the breed based on sanctioned Lure Field Trial results from the provisional recognition period. If the Annual Convention of Delegates does not approve full recognition, it may vote to extend the provisional recognition period until the next Annual Convention of Delegates; such extension shall require a two-thirds majority vote of the Delegates present and voting.

Section 7. Revocation of Recognition. Once a breed is recognized as eligible to enter ASFA-sanctioned Lure Field Trials, this eligibility may be revoked only if:

(a) the Board of Directors recommends that a breed be removed from the list of eligible breeds, and

(b) an Annual Convention of Delegates, held not less than six months later than the Board recommendation, votes by a two-thirds majority of Delegates present to revoke the breed's eligibility.

(c) In such cases, the breed will be removed from the list of eligible breeds on January 1 of the following year.

Amendments

Section 1. Amendments to the Constitution and By-Laws may be proposed by the Board of Directors, by a special committee appointed by a Convention of Delegates for such purpose, or by a written petition addressed to the Corresponding Secretary signed by the Club Delegates of one-third of the member clubs in good standing. Amendments proposed by such petition shall be promptly considered by the Board of Directors and must be submitted with recommendations of the Board of Directors for a vote at the next Annual Convention of Delegates held at least forty-five (45) days after receipt of the petition or at a Special Convention of Club Delegates properly requested by the petitioners.

Section 2. The Constitution and By-Laws may be amended by a two-thirds majority vote of the member clubs present and voting at such Annual Convention of Delegates or Special Convention of Club Delegates, provided the proposed amendments have been mailed to each Club Delegate at least thirty (30) days prior to the date of such convention.

ARTICLE XI
Order of Business

Section 1. At Annual Conventions of Delegates of the Association, the order of business, so far as the character and nature of the meetings may permit, shall be as follows:

(a) Roll call and seating of Delegates
(b) Minutes of the last Annual Convention of Delegates and Special Conventions of Delegates since the last Annual Convention of Delegates
(c) Report of the President
(d) Report of the Vice Presidents
(e) Report of the Recording Secretary

(f) Report of the Corresponding Secretary

(g) Report of the Treasurer

(h) Reports of the Committees

(i) Amendments to the Constitution and By-Laws

(j) Amendments to the *Running Rules and Field Procedures— Lure Field Trials*

(k) Unfinished business

(l) New business

(m) Election of Officers

(n) Adjournment

Section 2. At meetings of the Board of Directors, the order of business, unless otherwise directed by majority vote of those present, shall be as follows:

(a) Minutes of the last meeting and report of matters handled by mail

(b) Report of the Recording Secretary

(c) Report of the Corresponding Secretary

(d) Report of the Treasurer

(e) Reports of the Committees

(f) Unfinished business

(g) New business

(h) Adjournment

Section 3. Parliamentary Authority. The rules contained in the current edition of *Robert's Rules of Order, Newly Revised* shall govern the Association in all cases to which they are applicable, but only when they are not inconsistent with this Constitution and By-Laws and any special rules of order the Association may adopt. A Parliamentarian shall be elected at each of the Association's meetings.

ARTICLE XII

Dues and Fees

All dues and fees, unless otherwise stipulated, shall be determined at and by Conventions of Delegates.

ARTICLE XIII

Dissolution

The Association may be dissolved at any time by the written consent of not less than two-thirds of the member clubs. In the event of dissolution of the Association, whether voluntary or involuntary or by operation of law, none of the property of the Association nor any proceeds thereof nor any assets of this Association shall be distributed to any member of the Association but, after payment of the debts of the Association, its property and assets shall be given to a charitable organization for the benefit of dogs, selected by the Board of Directors.

APPENDIX TO THE CONSTITUTION AND BY-LAWS

The following items are policies established by the Board of Directors and ratified by an Annual Convention of Delegates; however, they are not part of the Constitution of the Association.

Article III. Affiliation

Section 3. Fees associated with an application for Affiliation will not be refunded if a club is denied Affiliation.

Article VI. The Association Year, Annual Convention of Delegates, Nominations

Section 4(d). A National Club shall be represented in the region of residence of its Club Delegate.

5

Getting Started in Lure Coursing

THE FIRST THING you need to get started in lure coursing is a sighthound that will chase the "bunny." This sounds simple, but not every sighthound will run just because someone wants it to. Your hound must also be reliable off leash because even a track star couldn't keep up with most sighthounds in full stride.

LURE-COURSING CLUBS—FINDING OR FOUNDING

If you attend a trial or a practice and discover that this is a sport that your hound actually enjoys, your next step is to find a club within driving distance so you can start competing. Your best bet for this is to subscribe to *Field Advisory News* (*FAN*), the official magazine of the ASFA, or to the *AKC Lure Coursing Newsletter*. The latter has a list of trials for both groups, while *FAN* only lists those run by ASFA. However, *FAN* publishes a list of clubs all over the country that are active in trials. If you are fortunate enough to find a club near you, join it and offer to help out in any way that you can. As you gain knowledge of the various jobs, it will help you as well as the club.

In lure-coursing trials, the lure operator works from a ladder. The motor, wheel and string are all essential items of equipment. The lure is actually a white plastic trash bag. Also seen here are the huntmaster and two competitors and their Scottish Deerhounds.

Most clubs offer practices after their trials and some even schedule practice sessions on certain weekends where members run their hounds free and nonmembers pay a nominal fee. Find one of those and you're in business.

However, if your situation is like mine, and you live at least three hours from any trial-giving club, you might want to do what my wife and I did—start your own lure-coursing group. I'll tell you how we started and then you can take it from there.

When I began attending lure-coursing trials in 1986 and saw that my Salukis were thoroughly enjoying themselves, the first thing I thought of was practice. It's one thing driving 300 miles to an actual trial, but it's much too far to travel for practice sessions. We are fortunate in having enough open land—about four acres—to set up a practice course of about 500 yards.

THE EQUIPMENT

The next thing needed was equipment. At one of the trials, we were advised to contact Tom Bianchi of Injoy Wood Products in Charlotte, Vermont, who makes all the equipment we would need. As a result, we ordered a lure machine, six corner pulleys to set up a practice course, and a hold-down pulley that is used to keep the string from riding too high.

Other essentials include at least one 600-yard spool of nylon cord and preferably two if you mess things up (easy to do). You will also need spikes to nail the pulleys and the motor to the ground. You will have a continuous loop wheel that the cord will ride on and a takeup reel to wind the cord back up when you're finished running your dog. You'll also need some white plastic bags to use as lures and at least one strong battery to run the motor of the lure machine. All the equipment you need to get started will probably cost about $400.

When we started our club, we used the equipment we had, but as we made a bit of money on each trial, we added more pulleys and string, along with other essentials and luxuries. We have been in business since 1989, and as this is being written we're just about ready to purchase equipment for the club.

A motor and continuous loop wheel.

This motor is fitted with a takeup reel to remove the string from the course.

Motor and stand showing shaft for wheels.

RUNNING A TRIAL

Here is how we started our club. We had four experienced lure coursers. One knew the paperwork, the three others had coursed at many trials (and one of these was an experienced judge who knew everything about machinery and setting up lure courses).

With these, plus a couple of novices who were eager to learn, we set up shop. The only thing the novice lure courser actually needs to start running is a dog that will course, a set of racing blankets (bright yellow, bright pink and bright blue) and a slip lead to slip the hound when the huntmaster gives the *tallyho*! As a new club, we attracted a goodly number of novices who wanted to see whether or not their sighthounds would chase the plastic lures. Those whose hounds wouldn't usually lost interest and those whose hounds did stayed on in the club. Your membership will be constantly changing and you will be breaking in new people all the time. Even with a growing membership, the bulk of the work in running our trials was still on the backs of our original four members. In fact, at the time of our last trial one of those four unfortunately had to move out of the area and I learned what it meant to take up the slack. My wife and I staked out the first course the day before the trial—pacing off the course and putting in stakes where the pulleys are to go. This makes it easier for the person who actually lays out the course the morning of the trial. Then at a certain hour—usually 9 A.M.—inspection and roll call are announced. (This is noted in the premium list.) All entries must be checked for lameness, and the bitches are examined for signs of being in season. (Any found are excused and their owners' entry fees refunded.) After the judge or judges walk the course, a test dog is usually run to make sure the judge and lure operator can see the dogs over the entire course. Meanwhile, the order of running by breeds is posted along with the call names of contestants. At this point, the trial is ready to begin.

Once you get your feet wet, it's really not very difficult, and all the participants have a good time, especially the hounds. Care must be taken to ensure that your equipment is in top condition. Nothing holds up a lure trial like equipment failure. It is wise to have a backup motor and several extra solenoids handy in case something should stop working. Experienced contestants will look at the running order and usually have their dogs up waiting at the proper time. The huntmaster should have a list of dogs so he or she can check the names and blanket colors when the dogs come on line. The blanket colors are especially important because this is how the judges judge the hounds—on their colors. As each breed is finished, the judge or judges mark their sheets and send them back by

Hold-down pulley to keep string from riding high on uneven ground.

Corner pulley with spikes for fastening.

"Beating the gun."
Off to a good start.

At the end of the chase.

Gathering the hounds after
the run.

169

courier to the field secretary, who enters them on the record sheet. A copy of this sheet is then posted so the contestants can see how their hounds were scored. When the preliminary course is completed for all breeds, the course is reversed (the hounds run in the opposite direction) and the final course is started. After this, in ASFA trials the winner of the open stake runs against the winner of the field-champion stake for Best of Breed. Either of these dogs can forfeit to the other if the handlers don't want them to run. After this and tie-score runoffs are completed, there is another draw for Best in Field. Each Best of Breed dog is eligible but does not have to run. Those that do run are drawn in trios or duos and scored by the judges to determine Best in Field. This finale is especially important in AKC trials because the winner can pick up as many as five points.

There you have a graphic description of how a lure field trial is run. Your club must be sure to have enough ribbons, rosettes and usually trophies available to cover all the breeds and Best in Field. These are presented to the winners at the conclusion of the trial. Then comes more work for the field trial secretary. He or she must send a copy of the complete trial record to either the ASFA or the AKC, depending on which organization sponsored the trial. Both organizations also collect $3.00 for each dog that competes. All of this must be sent in usually within ten days. In this way, the winning dogs are credited with the number of points they receive depending on the entry in that particular breed. That is how champions are made.

For further information refer to the rules and regulations for lure-coursing programs in Chapter 4.

ON GROUNDS

If I had to select the most important aspect of running a successful trial, it would have to be the grounds. The lure trial field should cover at least five acres. It can be fairly hilly in spots, but a level field makes it much easier for the judges and lure operators to function. If possible, the boundaries should be wooded because hounds usually do not like to enter wooded areas, and there is less chance for them to take off. There should be ample space either on the field or off to park vehicles, and if you don't own the field be sure to clean up thoroughly at the end of each day so you can continue to use it. The photographs in this chapter will give you some idea of what the equipment looks like and how it is set up. *Tallyho!*

6

Conditioning Sighthounds for Lure Coursing

WE'RE GOING TO START this chapter with sound management during puppyhood and the first item of vital importance is feeding. I have had a theory for many years on why the life span, especially of the larger sighthound breeds, has been shrinking. Some dog-food companies have been trying to enhance their products by increasing the amount of protein, vitamins and minerals that they have been incorporating into their formulations, especially the puppy formulations. As a result, the frames of bigger breeds such as Irish Wolfhounds and Scottish Deerhounds have been growing at a faster rate than the organs inside these dogs. The organs then have to work harder to sustain the frames and therefore wear out faster, resulting in shorter life spans. Be very careful what you feed your running hound— especially during the growth stage. Twenty-five years ago, before dog food became the major industry it is today, life spans of larger breeds were four to five years longer than they are today. We feed a quality puppy food but one with a sensible amount and balance of protein and vitamins. As our dogs mature and start to work, we add quality protein, such as eggs and cheese, to their diet. Feeding correctly is extremely important, especially in sighthounds that are intended to be used to hunt or course.

EXERCISE

Exercise is also an important factor in raising sighthounds that will eventually be coursed. A large, securely fenced area for them to run and exercise in is absolutely essential. For those who just won't exercise by themselves, we try to accustom them to *roading* as early in life as possible. In roading sessions, my wife sits on the tailgate of our station wagon with one of our Salukis following on a conventional leash and collar while I drive between five and ten miles an hour. Some hounds love it, others do not. I've noticed that starting a young dog along with one that is experienced helps considerably. We start for about a mile and gradually increase to three or four. My oldest Saluki, Red Fox, still roads for three miles a day except in very hot weather. He is well over eleven years of age. At this writing he is still coursing toward his LCM.

Another way to exercise hounds that don't like to road is to turn them loose in an open field each day, one at a time. I emphasize one at a time because two together are quite likely to take off for hours, while a singleton will usually run until it gets tired and then return to you.

TRAINING

Training a sighthound is easier than training a retriever. If a sighthound likes to chase the white plastic "bunny" it will—otherwise it probably won't. Most of my experience has been with Salukis, and I have found that when we breed two enthusiastic coursing hounds together, the puppies will usually show a desire to course. Otherwise they are a question mark. We start teasing the pups as early as ten weeks with a piece of white plastic attached to a fish line. After they chase it for a short period of time, I usually let them catch it. It is important not to overdo. Then, at six or seven months, I run them about 100 or 150 yards a couple of times. After that I try taking them to a trial where I am running other dogs, so they can watch. Then, at just under a year, we let them complete a short course. Some owners

Broad jumps and high jumps such as are normally used in AKC obedience trials are excellent aids in conditioning sighthounds for lure coursing — and the hounds love using them.

"Roading" on foot provides wonderful, healthful exercise for hounds and handler.

Any reasonably safe action games are excellent for conditioning sighthounds. This Saluki is, notwithstanding its heritage, getting excited about catching snowballs.

The well-conditioned hound will enjoy an edge when the huntmaster calls "Tally-Ho."

don't like to start running their hounds in competition until they are two years of age. I start as soon as possible after they reach a year.

I always promise myself that at an early age I will teach my Salukis to come when called. This is simple to do. When they reach the age of eight weeks or so, put your hound on a long line and call it. Use a reward when it comes and, with any luck, by the time it starts coursing, you won't have nearly as much trouble as I do in retrieving my hounds at the end of a course. You see, I always promise myself, but I never get to it!

With eleven hound breeds ranging from very large to quite small, it's hard to generalize as to what kind or amount of exercise is right for all the breeds. Something that you might do with a Saluki you might not want to do with a Basenji or even a Whippet. My experience is with Scottish Deerhounds and Greyhounds besides Salukis, and I have found that they all have trained about the same. My last Greyhound came right off the track and, at first, he would not chase from a slip lead. Then it dawned on me that he had been used to breaking out of a box at the track. My wife then took him out to the middle of our practice course and took off his leash. I ran the lure past him and she uttered words of encouragement. The first time he took a few tentative steps. Then I reversed the string and he finally took off. It was thrilling to see. Most of the track Greyhounds that I have seen seem to take to lure coursing easily. One thing to remember about this breed, though—the track races are never over 400 yards, while lure courses are considerably longer. Therefore they should be practiced more so that they will learn to pace themselves for the longer distance instead of constantly sprinting. I have also seen some appear to quit after the lure turns once or twice. The explanation for this is simple: They think the race is over. At the track the rabbit disappears when the race ends. If you slow the lure down in practice the Greyhound will soon learn to watch the lure and keep running. My Greyhound was a class-A racer that was finally disqualified for bumping. I never did cure that problem, although I've seen very little of it in other former track dogs that I have watched.

I am certainly still learning. With Salukis, we only run what we have bred and raised and so with them I am somewhat more aware of the problems to be encountered along the way. You might well use some of my experiences on your own hounds with success. Presently I have a couple of two-year-old hounds. One has both ASFA and AKC lure-coursing points and had never put a foot down wrong in his first trials. I then took him to three trials where he ran about half the course and suddenly took off, leading me on a merry chase. He never ventured far, but he did it the entire three days of the trial. The only think I could think of to do was to give him a respite from lure coursing and introduce him to the show ring. He's a good-looking Saluki, and maybe by the time he finishes his conformation championship he'll decide to run correctly once again. Besides Salukis, I have seen this problem in Ibizans, Pharaohs, and especially in Afghans, so at least I'm not alone. Many owners and handlers just give up and get another hound, but my mind does not run that way. I have trained too many retrievers, bird dogs and spaniels to ever give up as long as I think there is any hope, and with me there's always hope.

7

First Aid for
Sighthounds
in the Field

ALL ACTIVE CANINE-BASED sporting events—
hunting tests; field trials for retrievers, pointing dogs and spaniels;
Beagle, Basset and Dachshund trials; herding tests and any others not
mentioned here—contain a certain element of risk to the contestants.
The same is true of lure coursing trials. In one way there is more risk
because most contestants travel at high rates of speed and collisions
are not uncommon. On the other hand, the courses are examined
carefully by the judges and usually the lure operator before the trial
starts. In this way, the danger of the hounds stepping in a hole or
becoming entangled in barbed wire is minimal. However, there is a
small percentage of injuries to the hounds during the trials. In seven
years of coursing, my Salukis have had two rough collisions and a few
ripped pads but nothing more serious to worry about. The most common type of injury is burns from the string. Remember the strong nylon
cord is traveling at a high rate of speed to keep the lure in front of the
hounds, and if a dog gets tangled in the string, it could be cut badly.
However, the lure operators know this and will stop the lure and have

the string off the wheel in just a few seconds, thus minimizing cuts or burns. Sometimes a hound will try to grab the string and will cut its mouth in the process. Some hounds do this so often that they develop calluses in their mouths. On the rare occasion when a hound actually suffers a fracture, that is considered serious.

YOUR FIRST-AID KIT

Over the past forty years I have run various breeds of dogs in almost every type of performance event. During this time I have amassed a general first-aid kit to take care of most injuries on the spot. Here is what you will need. First, a waterproof plastic box. A fishing-tackle box is excellent. In it, put adhesive tape, preferably an inch in width; an ample roll of gauze bandage, three inches wide (two inches for whippets); a sterile gauze pad, three-by-three inches; scissors; and a splint. The splint is important. I use a rolled aluminum variety known as "Sam Splint," made by Jorgensen Laboratories in Loveland, Colorado. It is heavy enough to immobilize the bone or bones involved and is malleable enough to bend to almost any shape needed. Of course you must use gauze bandage before applying the splint. It is packed in rolls and the smaller paw splints would be excellent for Whippets. Remember, this is about first aid in the field. The idea is to immobilize the bones involved until you can get your hound to a veterinarian and have it X-rayed to determine the amount of damage. Many vets also use Sam Splint for permanent casts. Jorgensen Laboratories has also come out with a clear plastic tarsal splint designed for quick, accurate fitting. This is especially good if there are cuts and tears associated with the broken bones. The plastic is clear, and if windows are left in the bandage over the lesions, the lesions can be monitored while the break is healing. These two items are a must in my kit. You will probably never have to use them, but it's a nice feeling to know that they are there just in case!

The splints are especially important for Greyhounds and Whippets as they suffer the great majority of broken bones.

The next essential is 3-percent hydrogen peroxide. Include your choice of these useful preparations: antibacterial ointment, such as povidone-iodine, Bacitracin or triple antibiotic ointment. Furacin ointment or powder is also excellent, as is vitamin A & D ointment. Silver nitrate sticks, alum or styptic pencil are needed to stop bleeding. A

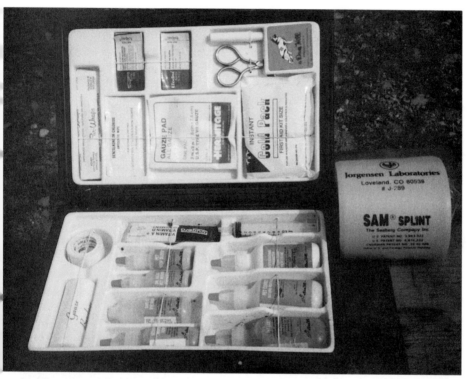

A well-equipped first-aid kit for hounds taking part in lure coursing. Also shown is the "Sam Splint" mentioned in the text.

There are many safety hazards in the normal lure-coursing field. For example, external parasites will always be a factor. They can be especially troubling for Afghans and other longhaired hounds.

good, safe eyewash is important for obvious reasons. Boric acid was once considered best, but recent research has proven it too harsh. Happily, there are many safe, effective eye preparations on the market. Other equipment and supplies you need for your first-aid kit include K-Y jelly or other sterile lubricant, a chemical ice pack or plastic freezer bags for ice, tweezers, mineral oil, a thermometer (I use the instant model with a big dial), a 12-cc syringe for oral medication, an eyedropper, Karo syrup or other high-energy formula, Q-Tips or other sterile cotton-tip applicator sticks, wire cutters or needle-nose pliers and Betadine solution or wound powder.

With all of the foregoing you should have everything needed to treat almost any kind of injury that a hound could sustain in the field. Always remember to try quieting your hound if it's in pain and ascertaining the injury before you attempt to move it. Even if it is snapping, don't muzzle it unless absolutely necessary. It will only increase its panic. Try to calm it, and stay calm yourself. Some hounds tend to be big babies and will scream at the slightest simple string burn while others will continue running as though nothing is wrong. Always examine your hound carefully after it has been tangled in the string. Even a slight cut can become infected if it is not treated promptly. If your hound comes back to you after running a course shaking its head, check its ears carefully for foreign matter or some type of small insect. Always remember that the hound is your responsibility and it is coursing because you want it to.

DEALING WITH TICKS

This might not come under the heading of first aid, but I think it's important enough to include in this chapter. Ticks do not live in every section of the country yet, but they're getting there. If you course your dog in any section of the South, or even in the East, ticks can be a menace. If you are coursing far from home, always ask one of the local contestants whether you need to watch for ticks. Remember also that sighthounds can have bad reactions to many of the chemicals used to kill ticks, so be careful about what you use. I use a product called Natra spray that can be used on your hound as many times as you wish without danger. It contains pyrethrins but leaves no residue. You must actually hit the tick to kill it. During the day, where there are ticks around I try to exercise my hounds on flat ground. On roadsides, keep

The practice of inspecting hounds before going to the line can reveal an unsuspected injury or a temporary lack of soundness. In such cases it would be better for such hounds not to make a run at all.

Whippets have tremendous heart but relatively thin skins, and they can come up with some nasty injuries. Owners should take extra precautions as needed.

your hound away from high bushes or other heavy vegetation. Ticks tend to climb bushes and then fall off onto passing people and animals. The common dog tick is bad enough, but now we're also dealing with the deer tick, the tiny carrier of Lyme disease. This species is much smaller than other ticks and hard to detect. After a day of coursing I go over my Salukis carefully, starting with the pads of the feet and the feathering. I spray every portion with Natra spray. I work until the entire dog has been thoroughly sprayed. If a tick remains embedded after being sprayed I simply leave it to drop off when it dies. If I see the tick before spraying and want to be sure it is completely removed, I either touch it with a hot match head to make it back out or put some oil on it to smother it. If ticks can't breathe they will also back out. In this way its nasty pincers do not stay in your hound to cause infection. With care, you can keep your hound free from ticks and save yourself considerable worry. The vaccine for Lyme disease has been approved but I have seen too many dogs have an allergic reaction to it and actually show symptoms of the disease. Sighthounds are so unusually sensitive to so many chemicals that I would hesitate to use this vaccine. I'd rather cope with the ticks and any other bugs around the area myself. If you are careful, you have a reasonable chance of keeping your dog free of these monsters. Just remember that sighthounds are especially sensitive to many of the remedies used on other breeds. Be careful. If your hound has to have a general anesthetic for any reason, make sure that you warn the veterinarian to go easy on the amount. I have seen too many hounds lost needlessly from a simple operative procedure when the veterinarian is not familiar with their tolerance levels for anesthetics.

In the foregoing I have given you most of the material you will need to keep your hound healthy and safe while it enjoys itself lure coursing.

Tschida's Willie Nelson, F. Ch., CC, a Saluki owned by Bonnie Schulz, was the winner of the 1984 International Invitational.

Since its inception in September 1991, AKC lure coursing has been a complete success. Sighthound fans such as these have made the sport an important phase of the performance events program.

8

History of the ASFA
International Invitational
and the AKC
Inaugural Trials

ALTHOUGH THE ASFA lure-coursing program was initiated in 1972, it was not until 1978 that the first International Invitational was held. This trial was designed to run as an annual event in a different location of the United States from year to year. The first running saw seventy-one sighthounds compete at DuQuoin, Illinois. Best in Field was captured by a Scottish Deerhound, Fairyfort's Highland Fling, owned by J. Mayo.

Before the 1979 running, there were several changes in the eligibility requirements. Hounds had to have acquired at least twenty points during the preceding twelve months, have placed in a Regional Invitational, and be a field champion of record or have the equivalent in foreign requirements.

The 1979 International Invitational came east to New Jersey, at Duke Island Park. There were seventy-five entered, and Best in Field was won by a Whippet, Timbar's Saturn Sun Maid, owned by L. and S. Spiga.

In 1980, the International Invitational moved out to Chino, California, and the entry fell to fifty-seven dogs. Best in Field was the Saluki Sirahare Bathsheba, LCM, owned by J. Stake.

The year 1981 saw the International Invitational move to Spencer, Iowa, and it was the first to stretch over two days. There were actually two trials, one each day of the Invitational, with eighty-two dogs entered each day. There was no Best in Field awarded, only Bests of Breed for each day.

The 1982 International Invitational returned to the East Coast and was held at Amherst, Massachusetts, where a steady rain greeted the hounds and handlers on both days. Best in Field was garnered by the Saluki Azad Shaitan Wahad, Can. F. Ch., owned by J. and R. Preiss.

In 1983, the International Invitational moved down to Bethlehem, Pennsylvania, where it saw a large entry of 264 compete during the two days. Best in Field was taken by the Whippet Bitterblue's Castle Fire, owned by S. Silloway and L. Garwacki.

In 1984, the International Invitational moved once again to the Midwest. It was held in Stillwater, Minnesota, and again had a large entry of 208 hounds. Best in Field was the Saluki Tschida's Willie Nelson, owned by Bonnie Schulz. It is interesting to note that of the Bests in Field awarded in the first six International Invitationals, three were taken by Salukis, two by Whippets, and one by a Scottish Deerhound.

In 1985 the International Invitational again moved east, this time to Lewisberry, Pennsylvania, where the entry rose to 244. A Borzoi finally crashed in for Best in Field. This trailblazer, Windhound's Zip, LCM, was owned by A. and L. Lillstrom.

The 1986 International Invitational inched a bit farther west to a staging point at Ravenna, Ohio. A huge entry of 279 competed over the two-day span, with the Whippet Buncrana's Fullerton, F. Ch., emerging as the choice for Best in Field. He was owned by P. McLaughlin.

The International Invitational moved to Kansas City, Missouri, for the 1987 running and boasted an entry of 260 hounds. Best in Field was taken by a Saluki, Ch. Mashalla David's Arwa, F. Ch., owned by T. and S. Shuman. This moved the Saluki one win up on the Whippet for Bests in Field. This was also the year that the Afghan Hound Caravan's Rhythm N' Blues, F. Ch., owned by Amy and Phil Peake, took Best of Breed both days and ended up as the top coursing

Any effort, to be successful, depends on dedicated workers. These happy movers and shakers deserve full marks for their part in the AKC Labor Day lure-coursing trials in 1992. Shown with this group are Dean Wright, AKC Coursing Director (second from right), and Robert McKowen, AKC Vice President of Performance Events (at far right).

The Best of Breed trophies offered at the AKC inaugural trial on Labor Day, 1991, added their own luster to the prestige of the historic occasion.

Afghan in the country. I had the pleasure of watching her run many times.

The International Invitational has to be held either on the first weekend in June or during the month of January, and 1988 was the first International Invitational to be held in January. It was held in La Marque, Texas, and the 190 hounds and handlers enjoyed good weather throughout the two days. Best in Field was again garnered by a Saluki, this one Henrad Conan, owned by J. Adams.

In 1989, the International Invitational resumed its normal pattern of the first weekend in June. It was held in Rougemont, North Carolina. Best in Field came as a surprise, with the Basenji Stilwell's Ben Hur capturing top honors of Best in Field. He was owned by Stromberg and DeWhitt. The total entry was a large 259 over the two days.

In 1990, the thirteenth International Invitational shifted to Hanover, Pennsylvania, and it was the first International Invitational that I actually attended. The tension that is put on both dogs and handlers must be experienced. Best in Field was corralled by the Greyhound Treybeau's Fantasy, LCM V, owned by Dean and Sandy Wright. I was running two Salukis, Black Brant's Peerless Peanut in the open and Black Brant's Red Ruffian in the field champion stake. On the first day, Peanuts tied for first and went to runoff with the other open and the field-champion stake winner. I messed him up and he ended up coming in second. Sunday, however, was a different story. He won the open stake by a narrow margin and then defeated the field champion winner for Best of Breed, also finishing his field-champion title at the same time. I was understandably excited; it was an unforgettable thrill. Among the nineteen Salukis entered, he defeated seven of the top lure coursers in the country and he was not yet two years old. He made a good run for Best in Field but couldn't quite make it. There were 185 hounds entered each day, or a total of 370. That was quite a weekend.

In 1991, the International Invitational again went west, this time near Denver, Colorado. I tried to get there but couldn't quite make it. The entry was down to 119 hounds that year, with just 4 Salukis. However, Montebello Sherom's Fuhais, LCM II, made up for that by taking the coveted Best in Field award.

The year 1992 was a nightmare for me. I actually made it down to Lexington, Kentucky, for the running of the fifteenth International Invitational. I ran both my Salukis, first Red Fox and then Peanuts. The latter decided he wanted to see more of Kentucky and I actually had to chase him for almost three miles before getting him to jump into his crate. My legs were so tired that I couldn't compete the next

Lyle Gillette, the father of modern lure coursing (center), visits with Dean Wright (left) and Robert McKowen (right) at the AKC inaugural trial.

Ken Marden (foreground) handles a Whippet at the line at the 1992 AKC trial.

day. It was a long trip home. Best in Field was won by the Whippet Finghin's Wandering Joe, owned by John and Pat Mattox and Elaine McMichael.

The American Kennel Club has been operating for well over a hundred years and has licensed and sanctioned all types of performance events in addition to dog shows, but it wasn't until September 1991 that the AKC sponsored its first set of lure coursing trials for sighthounds. The trials were held at Hanover Shoe Farms in Hanover, Pennsylvania, and were hosted by the Mason-Dixon Ibizan Hound Club. Sixty-five hounds competed on Saturday, seventy on Sunday and seventy-seven on Monday, for a total of two hundred twelve over three days. Saturday saw the Irish Wolfhound Megan Turbo Espirit, owned by Robert O'Gorman, take Best in Field. Sunday, the Ibizan Hound Smotare's Bramblewood Lizard, owned by Judy and Peter Parker, took top honors, while the Labor Day event saw the Scottish Deerhound Vale Vue Gelin of Bellanagare, owned by Norma and Bob Sellers, beat the other seventy-six hounds.

A summary of the AKC lure coursing for its first year of operation saw twenty-four all-breed and ten specialty field trials held. There were also a total of fifty-seven Junior Courser tests. AKC points were earned by 115 hounds in 1991, while 257 earned their Junior Courser titles. Two hundred hounds also earned their Senior Courser titles. Only four hounds—an Afghan, an Ibizan, a Pharaoh and a Borzoi—became AKC field champions that year.

The year 1992 saw a dramatic increase in the number of AKC trials and tests. In all sections of the United States, clubs formed by the ASFA were trying out the AKC format. The AKC tests were especially popular, not only with prospective participants but for owners of potentially aggressive hounds. These owners could still receive a Junior Courser to prove their dog could at least chase the bunny. Many Senior Coursing titles were also awarded up to Labor Day 1992. The main effect of the AKC program was to interest many sighthound owners in participating in hound activities other than conformation competition. As sighthounds are not the epitome of virtue in obedience competition, this left lure coursing as the happy alternative, at least for the hounds.

Although ASFA supporters were worried that the new program would deplete the number of their own lure coursing trials, this has not proven to be the case. The number of ASFA trials actually increased during the first year of AKC lure coursing. Many clubs scheduled ASFA trials and AKC tests on the same weekends and benefited from

Cameo's Gone with the Wind, F. Ch., an Afghan Hound owned by Bonnie Schulz, was Best of Breed at the International Invitational in 1991 and 1992.

A fraction of the vehicles and some of the attendees at the AKC inaugural lure-coursing trial in 1991.

the added revenue taken in on the tests. So far, both programs have benefited people interested in lure coursing and increased their number dramatically.

It is my hope that in the future the two organizations will come to a mutual understanding that will benefit not only the organizations but the sport of lure coursing and, most of all, the sighthounds, which obviously derive so much enjoyment from "chasing the bunny."

Both ASFA and AKC publish excellent, informative periodicals for the information and education of lure-coursing enthusiasts. As this book goes to press, further information can be obtained from these sources:

FIELD ADVISORY NEWS
Vicky Clarke, Editor
P.O. Box 399
Alpaugh, CA 93201

AKC COURSING NEWS
Larry Flynn, Editor
R.D. 1, Box 1733
Stewartstown, PA 17363

Tschida's Willie Nelson, F. Ch., CC, displaying the form and drive that fueled his success in lure coursing. *Garry Newton*

9

Lure Coursing in Canada

by Lin Jenkins

THIS BOOK is well served by this chapter by Lin Jenkins. Lin has been active in lure coursing for the past eleven years and has coursed Salukis, Greyhounds and Whippets. She is also a Saluki breeder, using the Lorrequer prefix, and was the breeder and owner of the number-two and number-three Salukis in 1991.

In addition, Lin is a fully licensed coursing judge for all breeds. She has judged extensively in Quebec, in Ontario and in the eastern United States.

TALLYHO! CANADIAN STYLE

Lure Coursing came to Canada in 1976 through the efforts of Heather and Jeff Loube and Jan Priddy and friends. Heather and Jeff had been interested in coursing for a year or so, having tried a primitive form of it in their backyard in 1975 with a bicycle and "broomstick" pulleys. They soon gave up on this exercise because the line kept getting tangled irretrievably in the bicycle, and the "broomsticks" were constantly being decapitated. So they made trips across the

Chris Williams (foreground) and Judy Snider slipping their exuberant Afghans.

border to the United States to participate in the sport, but they were hooked. In 1976, they took out an ad in a Victoria, British Columbia, newspaper to see if there was anyone out there as interested as they were. One of the first people to respond was Helena James—of Ringdove Whippets—who had recently arrived in Canada from England. A high school teacher volunteered to undertake the construction of the equipment as a school project, and the first-ever lure coursing practice took place in the Loubes' backyard. Practice continued every Sunday morning from spring through summer, and as Heather was later to say, they made every mistake imaginable—but they were hooked.

At the end of the summer, it was decided to hold an official lure coursing trial. But there were major decisions to be made: Under what rules should they run? Could they run under ASFA rules? Where would they hold the trial? It was suggested they get an ASFA coursing club to sponsor the trial, but as the nearest club at that time was over 900 miles away, that idea was discarded. Eventually, it was decided to run on Thanksgiving weekend under ASFA rules and to arbitrarily call themselves the Canadian Sighthound Field Association (CSFA). At this time, however, the matter of the Canadian Kennel Club (CKC) was raised. How would they view this new sport? Would they look favorably on what CKC members were doing? They had a quick consultation with the CKC director for the area and were told that, provided they did not conflict with any other CKC event on that weekend, they could go ahead with their plans. The manager for shows and trials, Norman Brown (now retired), was also consulted. He was happy to help as he had been instrumental in drawing up the CKC constitution, which included provision for coursing! In the 1930s, "coursing" meant what we now call open-field coursing. However, he advised that they continue to operate and, once they felt they had something viable on a national basis, CKC should be approached again for guidance.

Judges were drawn from the United States. Ken and Vanelle Reynolds had already said they would be happy to help and they, together with Fred Schmietow from San Jose, California (who at that time owned the top Afghan), drove up in a rented motor home with a stop to pick up John Shook, then ASFA recording secretary, who had flown into Seattle from Denver.

The original site for the trial was canceled a week before the trial was due to be held, but a perfect replacement was found on the country estate of the Woodward family on Vancouver Island, British Columbia,

A Canadian Pharaoh Hound "slicing the wind."

where the Woodwards entertained their weekend guests with tours of the coursing field in the rain! The day of the trial dawned foggy—thick fog—necessitating a three-hour wait until it lifted enough to run the dogs and see where they were.

And Canadian lure coursing was off and running. From this little spark of interest, the sport spread rapidly across the country. The year 1977 saw Vancouver Island Coursing Association (VISA) hold two sets of trials, and the new Lower Mainland Sighthound Association held two sets also. Jan Priddy designed and donated the CSFA logo, Bonnie Goebel volunteered to keep the records (a position she still holds at this writing) as well as naming *CANFAN*, with Linda Buchholz and Heather Loube as editors. Also in 1977, the Loubes were transferred east to the Ottawa Valley Region. Upon arrival, they found themselves in the thick of organizing more coursing clubs. Ann Webster from British Columbia was in Ottawa that same year visiting family, and she had brought along a film on coursing. This became instrumental in the formation of the Capital Area Sighthound Association. Present at the viewing of the film was a Whippet fancier from the Montreal area, Everett Dansereau, and he soon persuaded the Loubes to go to Montreal with the film and help get things going in Quebec.

Nineteen seventy-eight was a volatile, exciting year for coursing in Canada. The Lower Mainland Sighthound Association failed to complete one of its spring trials, with the result that another club, the Fraser Valley Sighthounders, was formed. The Ontario Lure Coursing Association held its first and only trial. This club was later to re-form with new members and runs very successful trials today. The Cowichan Valley Lure Coursing Association, formed on Vancouver Island in 1977, held its first trials in 1978, and the newly formed Quebec Lure Coursing Assocation proved that coursing is possible even when it's snowing!

In the early years, Canadian coursers relied heavily on Americans, especially for judging. Without the help and enthusiasm of folks such as the Reynoldses, the Hayeses, the Bells, the Forresters and Dean Wright, Canadian coursing would surely have foundered on the rocks of inexperience. The Americans didn't just come to judge, either: They helped with equipment, huntmastered and field-clerked, ran their dogs and provided endless hours of posttrial advice and entertainment.

On April 9, 1977, at Royal Roads Military College, Victoria, British Columbia, the first Canadian field champion titles were completed—by two Afghans. One, Damien, was owned by Victoria Thom-

Am. & Can. Ch. Lorrequer Saklani Bekha, Am. & Can. CD, F. Ch.X., a Saluki owned by Ghislaine Lemieux and bred by Lin Jenkins, is a heart-stopping hound from any angle. The performance of such magnificent animals has fired many imaginations on both sides of the border and made many new friends for lure coursing.

son, and the other, Begum el Bamian, was owned by F. and H. Schmietow. The first Whippet field championship was also awarded that weekend—to Windwood Zip Code, owned by Bonnie Goebel. A number of other breed firsts followed—the first Canadian field champion Saluki was El Char's Al Qahirah Isis, owned by the Malones; the first Greyhound was Ch. Windwood Vent d'Hiver, bred and owed by Ann Webster. In 1978, the first Scottish Deerhound to become a Canadian field champion was Ailsa of Garryoaks, owned by the Smeetons, followed by the first Borzoi, Buffalo Joe, owned by the Redmans.

A quick look at trial results in *CANFAN* for the period 1977–78 shows there were a few breeds running consistently, notably Afghans, Borzois, Whippets, Greyhounds, Salukis and Scottish Deerhounds. One notable first occurred in 1978, when the first American, Canadian Bermudian bench champion won a field title. This was the Saluki Omega's Vallauris of Elana, owned by Nel Hyde. He was also the first Quebec field champion. At the end of this same year, the first field champion excellent was awarded to an Afghan—Ch. Sidney's Rocky Raccoon, Am. & Can. F. Ch., owned by Bob and Jackie Sinclair.

In December 1977, the CSFA elected executive officers, and their primary duty was to come up with some rules for Canadian coursing, using the ASFA rule book as a guideline. These rules were put into immediate effect and were the basis for future trials. They were basically the same as ASFA rules—the point awards were the same, the stakes were open and field champion (with Best in Field, time permitting). Mixed stakes were also offered to those breeds competing where there was not enough competition in the breed (i.e., only one or two) to warrant a full course. The executive body consisted of Heather Loube, president; Heather Higson, secretary, and Doug Philpott, treasurer, with *CANFAN* under the care of Linda Buchholz and Jan Priddy. There were three regional directors, in Alberta, British Columbia and Ontario.

CANFAN was being printed quarterly and was to prove invaluable to everyone who was interested in this new sport. The periodical was full of ideas, course plans and even full-color advertisements. In 1979, the first issue of the *CANFAN Annual*, under the editorship of Jan Priddy, was issued and it is still a keenly awaited annual, featuring the Top-Ten results. Finalization of the new Canadian Coursing Rule Book and completion of the Constitution for the CSFA both came in 1979. Under the chairmanship of Don Shafer, a system of judge licensing was put into effect, incorporating a reciprocal agreement with ASFA.

A beautiful Canadian Borzoi at full extension.

A Greyhound courser wearing a wire muzzle.

Until this time, the main problem with conducting trials was finding judges and enough knowledgeable people to do the various jobs associated with the sport. In the first years, as mentioned above, Canadian coursers relied on the American coursing fraternity to help out, but as the years went by, people soon learned how to huntmaster, lure-operate (and build lure machines), do the paperwork and all the other tasks that go along with the sport. Soon, too, people were brave enough to take up the challenge of judging and, by the end of 1979, the CSFA boasted eight fully licensed judges and three provisionals. Thirteen member clubs were formed in those early years, a good sign that coursing was up and running.

In 1979, the first Ibizan Hound coursing title was awarded to Gallantree's Eagle of Treybeau, LCM, owned by Dean Wright, and the first Pharaoh title went to Ch. Val-Ed's Amenemhet, LCM, and Ch. Beltara's Mister Futura, LCM, both owned by the Reeses.

During these first few years of trial and error, there were suggestions that the CKC should take coursing under its wing. This suggestion met with its fair share of detractors as well as supporters. However in 1981, under the leadership of Heather Loube, a more determined effort was launched to get the CKC to take over the sport. An approach was made to the CKC and a committee was formed, led by John Ross (Counterpoint Salukis), with members being drawn from across Canada. A study of the rule book was undertaken to decide what rule changes would be required to bring coursing in line with CKC policies. The proposed revisions were published in the March 1981 issue of *Dogs in Canada* (the CKC equivalent of *Pure-Bred Dogs—American Kennel Gazette*). One stumbling block was the recognition of Ibizan Hounds, as they were not a CKC-recognized breed and would, therefore, be ineligible to course under CKC rules. Another problem involved Pharaohs as the CKC did not recognize the Pharaoh Hound Club of America (PHCA), nor did it recognize the National Greyhound Association (NGA) or Indefinite Listing Privilege (ILP) numbers. A plus for Basenji breeders was that as the Basenji was a CKC-recognized sighthound, it would be eligible to course. The negotiations continued through 1981 and 1982, with the CKC eventually informing CSFA (in 1982) that the CKC would sanction lure coursing trials as official events.

Bonnie Goebel was asked by the CKC to continue to attend to records and to help the CKC staff understand how these records were kept. Bonnie is still the CSFA records chairperson, and without her

A Canadian Irish Wolfhound homing in on the lure.

A Scottish Deerhound in a hard-charging performance for Best in Field at a Canadian lure-coursing trial.

unfailing devotion to record keeping, lure coursing would not be what it is today. Heather Loube was the driving force behind lure coursing in Canada from its inception and through its formative years. By September of 1983, however, she felt it was time someone else took the reins, and she resigned as president. The position passed on to Barbara Parr Smith, and with this changeover, the CSFA passed into another new era, where the executive was changed every two years to ensure that new blood was at the helm.

By this time, too, *CANFAN* had evolved into its present 8½- by 11-inch format, and more people were being introduced to this wonderful sport. The list of approved and provisional judges had grown to the point that Canada was less dependent on American judges, although they were still used and welcomed to trials across Canada. Lure operators, huntmasters and secretaries were being trained on a regular basis, and lure coursing was in good hands. The CKC had set up a Lure Coursing Council under the leadership of British Columbia director Bud Haverstock, with members of this Council being drawn from clubs across the country. This Council had regular meetings to update rules and policies.

Each province has its own unique set of problems when it comes to putting on a trial. British Columbia can be plagued with rain, soggy fields and fog. Alberta and the Prairie provinces, while blessed with large open spaces in which to run dogs, get very hot, dry weather. Quebec's season is very short because it lacks available fields. Once the snow leaves and the fields dry out, there are precious few short weeks before the grass starts to grow, and farmers are reluctant to lend out their crop fields. Ontario courses, on the other hand, have a longer season because they have an abundance of provincial parks. Many of the "oldies" in the sport fondly reminisce about the Quebec Lure Coursing Association (QLCA) trial, with its hundreds of thousands (it seemed that way at the time) of mosquitoes, which plagued both dogs and handlers, and the other QLCA trial that was run in snow with black plastic bags as lures and dogs that thought we were all crazy. Other clubs farther west can claim the ultimate challenge of coursing—blue fingers, anoraks, mufflers, scarves and dog blankets on day one, to be followed the next day by shorts, T-shirts and sunscreen and hosing down dogs to keep them cool! The clubs that had been running the longest were getting bolder and more imaginative in their selection of trial sites, course plans and other particulars. Toronto lure coursers tried an "elimination event," where hounds were judged as in the English system: Two dogs ran together, with the winner determined by one judge who simply raised a flag to denote the winner and the winner progressing to the next "A," or winners' round, and the loser to "B," or the losers' round. Manitoba found "hills" for some of their trials. Although the hills were man-made (part of a city park), they made for challenging and varied courses. The Capital Area Sighthound Association (CASA) decided to go back to using the drag lure for one trial, utilizing two fields with a hedge separating them. Two openings were cut between the fields and the lure run through one, across a ditch, around the other field and back between another hole and up the hill to the finish. It was interesting to watch the veterans head down the hill toward the hedge, trying to outguess the lure because they knew for sure it would turn one way or another. After all, it always did, didn't it? Well, not so this time, much to their chagrin. The newcomers to the sport followed the lure straight through and generally fared better. Manitoba Gazehound Association approached Winnipeg Blue Bombers Football Club and offered to do a halftime show. It became quite a popular event and quite a challenge to put up a short course on the infield at halftime, parade the dogs, run the dogs and get out of there before the players came back on the field. Several clubs are now having sighthound specialties in conjunction with their local all-breed club championship shows, and many clubs put on demos at matches, specialty shows and "fun" days for the public to see what the sport is all about. In many instances, nonsighthound breeds are encouraged to give it a try, and some do very well indeed. Among the most outstanding breeds seen coursing were Giant Schnauzers, Dachshunds, Golden Retrievers and German Shepherd Dogs. If we were to follow this to its logical conclusion (if it chases a moving object, it's a sighthound), then all breeds would qualify!

By the 1986–87 season, CSFA started sending out certificates to the Top Ten Hounds in each breed, and these were also made retroactive to the start of coursing. Very soon thereafter, people started to get pleasant surprises in their mail as the certificates made their way across the United States and Canada. Some received certificates for dogs that had since passed away.

In the spring of 1987, the pioneers of coursing in Canada, Heather and Jeff Loube, advertised the start of the "Odyssey Cup." This was a knockout tournament and became an instant success.

The Whippet Ch. Devonair's Isabelle, F. Ch., owned by H. J. Dansereau, demonstrating that hounds *can* fly.

Sabine Beauman (foreground) and Lin Jenkins slipping their Whippet coursers. Intensity among humans and hounds is a shared thing.

There were no points awarded, but there were cash prizes for the first- and second-placed finishers. After Heather and Jeff retired, the Ontario Lure Coursing Association took over knockout coursing as part of its trial season, and it remains a popular event, bringing coursers from all over Canada and the United States to participate.

Coursing in Canada is now well established, and there is every reason to expect that it will continue to flourish. Some years are leaner than others. Trial numbers continue to fluctuate as some of the veterans leave, give up or simply retire from "doggy scenes." New people come along, give it a try and either become hooked or fade away. But the diehards continue to apply for dates; call judges; find fields and sit out in rain, sun, snow, or fog and do what we all love best—"chase the bunny."

For information on Canadian coursing, contact:

Secretary
 Susan Stewart
 P.O. Box 1479
 Ashcroft, BC V0K 1A0

CANFAN editor
 Linda Belleau
 R R #2, Nolalu
 ON P0T 2K0

Records Coordinator
 Bonnie Goebel
 27189 33 "A" Ave.
 Aldergrove, BC
 V0X 1A0

CSFA member clubs:
 Capital Area Sighthound Association (CASA)
 Gazehound Ontario (GO)
 Ibizan Hound Club of Canada
 Interior Gazehound Club
 Lower Mainland Whippet Association

A Canadian Ibizan Hound steaming down the course.

Three Lorrequer Salukis waiting to make magic in motion. They are (from left) Lorrequer Othello, F. Ch., Lorrequer Firuza Dubi, F. Ch., and Lorrequer Firuza Djahaina.

Manitoba Gazehound Association
Ontario Lure Coursing Association (OLCA)
Queon Lure Coursing Association (QLCA)
Toronto Lure Coursers (TLC)
True North Sighthound Association

CSFA-licensed lure coursing judges: 30, of whom 20 are all-breed

Can. Ch. Forerunner Blue Ribbon, F. Ch., a Whippet owned by Lin Jenkins.
G. C. Bayly

10

Making a
Dual Champion
the Hard Way

$\mathbf{I}$ THOUGHT I'd end this treatise on the sport of lure coursing by telling you how my Saluki, Dual Ch. Black Brant's Red Ruffian, popularly known as "Red Fox," attained his dual title. He is the first dog of any breed that my wife and I bred and that I handled to both his bench and field titles. This encompasses over forty-five years of trying. Red Fox is still going strong at the age of eleven and a half. He is still coursing regularly, and I show him at specialties in either the veterans or the Lure Coursing class. In fact, he won the latter class at the Empire Specialty in July 1992.

As I mentioned in the Preface, after an absence of over twenty years from the show ring, I took a look at Red Fox one day and decided that he was just too beautiful not to finish his bench championship. He was four and a half at the time. I had trepidation because the shows had changed so dramatically during my absence and I wasn't sure I could still handle successfully. Taking in a couple of shows put all my fears to rest. My red Saluki started in June and finished for his bench title in early October 1986. En route to his championship, he was

Dual Ch. Black Brant's Red Ruffian, owned by Arthur Beaman.

Winners Dog at the Empire Saluki Club summer specialty. This was his third show.

Shortly after he became a bench champion, the Empire Club held a "fun" field trial and asked whether I wanted to attend. This was the first time I had any inkling that there were field trials for sighthounds.

Red Fox ran the course twice quite successfully, and when I saw how happy this made him, and how pleased he was with himself, I decided, despite the fact that he was five years old, that he should have his chance to become a dual champion. In the spring of 1987, I began to enter him in lure coursing trials in addition to showing him on the bench. We were two busy people. He placed second in his first two trials and then, on his third try, he defeated the dog that had beaten him twice. He had Best of Breed that day, and I was very proud. The next weekend we had two BOBs in the show ring. I really had a dual-purpose Saluki. Then came his first accident. He had been running with a field champion that already had an LCM title and he was learning the ropes fast. This trial was in New England, and the course had several rather deep ditches running through it. Red Fox liked to jump these ditches, while his running mate chose to run through them. In the final course Red Fox gathered himself to jump when his opponent, honing in on the lure, ran into him, knocking him into the ditch. Red Fox hit his head on a rock and came out very wobbly. I took him back to my motel room and noted that his eyes weren't focusing correctly. He was better the next morning, but I decided to skip the second trial and return home. He recovered completely in a couple of weeks, but I discovered to my horror that he was now afraid of red Salukis. He wouldn't refuse to run, but he would run very wide, and that hurt him in the scoring. That was in early October. By the time the trial season ended in December he was getting over his phobia, but disaster struck again, and this time it was unrelated to coursing.

Red Fox loved to road behind our station wagon. My wife would sit on the tailgate holding him on leash while I drove the wagon between five and ten miles per hour. We usually used a little dirt road near our house, but this day it was quite muddy, so we switched to another, smaller road that was paved and clear. When we had traveled about a mile, a large mixed-breed dog came roaring out from behind a house and, with no warning, hit Red Fox on his blind side, ripping his groin from one end to the other. I didn't even know what had happened until my wife picked him up, put him in the car and told me to hightail it to our veterinarian.

Even after being stitched, the groin wound sustained by "Red Fox", as described in the text, was fearsome to see.

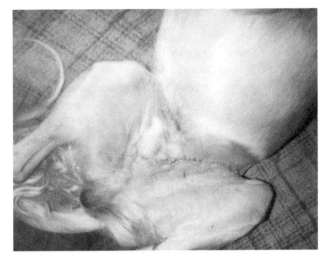

Arthur Beaman and "Red Fox," sharing a private moment. It took forty years, but in this hound Art had the dual champion he always dreamed of.

Lorraine Lilley

My prize Saluki ended up with thirty-two stitches and two drains in his undercarriage. Since the rip ended up in the inner portion of his leg, we had to carry him to and from his bed for him to take care of essential functions. Naturally he did not stay at our vet's, but as soon as he began to feel better and move around by himself, three or four of the stitches would pull out and it was back to the vet for resuturing. I thought he would never run again. Finally, after about four months, the wound had healed sufficiently for us to take him out with his brother and let him stretch his legs. We examined him closely afterward and he seemed to be whole once again. Remember this had not only taken him out of field trials but out of dog shows as well. In May 1988, he was well enough to take several big-breed wins, but I could see that his heart wasn't in it. He still wanted to run. So I entered him at two trials, and the quest for his field championship began once again. One blessing in disguise was that this traumatic experience had made him forget about his fear of red Salukis, and he and his red running mate were reunited once again. Finally, in early November 1988, he finished his field championship and became my first dual champion. It was a long, hard struggle and he had to have a great big heart and inordinate courage to continue running after all of his many misfortunes. In addition to the dual title, Red Fox has seventeen Bests of Breed on the bench as well as two Hound Group placements. Unfortunately, as he ran more in the field, he decided that the bench was no longer for him, and he stopped showing entirely. Even at his advanced age of eleven and a half, I still take him with me to some specialties. As long as he doesn't have to stay in the ring for too long he shows passably well. But when he's running in the field it is obvious that this is where his heart is. Coursing is the only sport that he really enjoys.

Red Fox is not alone. Look closely at some of the photographs in this book and note the ecstasy on the faces of these coursing sighthounds. You will see why more and more people are becoming active participants in this sport, especially those who want to keep their hounds both happy and healthy.